KISS AND RUN

THE **SINGLE, PICKY, AND INDECISIVE** GIRL'S GUIDE TO OVERCOMING HER FEAR OF COMMITMENT

ELINA FURMAN

A FIRESIDE BOOK
PUBLISHED BY SIMON & SCHUSTER

FIRESIDE
Rockefeller Center
1230 Avenue of the Americas
New York, NY 10020

The names and characteristics of some individuals in this
book have been changed.

FIRESIDE and colophon are registered trademarks
of Simon & Schuster, Inc.

For information regarding special discounts for bulk purchases, please contact
Simon & Schuster Special Sales at 1-800-456-6798
or business@simonandschuster.com.

Designed by Jan Pisciotta

Manufactured in the United States of America

10   9   8   7   6   5   4   3   2   1

Library of Congress Cataloging-in-Publication Data is available.

ISBN-13: 978-0-7432-8513-1
ISBN-10:   0-7432-8513-1

For Jay

Contents

Introduction

Who You Calling a Commitment-phobe?

For years, it was the men who had the monopoly on commitment-phobia. The stereotype of the ever elusive bachelor is perpetuated by such bestselling books as *Men Who Can't Love*, TV shows like *The Bachelor*, and magazine articles such as "Get Him to Pop the Question!" Men have been pegged as being out of touch with their emotions, holding out for their perfect dream girl, and running for the hills whenever women so much as mention the dreaded words *love* or *marriage*. No doubt about it—say "commitment-phobia" and most people automatically think "men."

But what about commitment-phobic women? Yes, women!

Raised to believe that men are the commitment-shy gender, many women coast through life completely oblivious to their own commitment anxiety—believing that they want a relationship yet systematically pushing away one perfectly suitable candidate after another.

With 47 million women currently single, it should come as no surprise that they are becoming as commitment-phobic as men. Women are taking longer and longer to settle down, putting off marriage in favor of work, starting their own businesses, and playing the field well into their thirties, forties, and fifties. Let's face it—many women can't even commit to a lunch date, let alone a lifelong relationship.

Still, with all the evidence of this growing trend, many people can't help wondering: *can women really be commitment-phobic?*

It never fails. At every party, dinner, and get-together, there is

at least one person who asks me that question, staring at me as if I'd just grown a horn in the middle of my forehead. Women *can't* be commitment-phobic, they say. After all, they're all far too busy planning fairy-tale weddings, picking out baby names, and scanning *Cosmo* for the "Top 10 Ways to Make Him Fall in Love."

But take Susan, for example. At 33, she's a successful event planner who has dated numerous men, broken many hearts (including that of an ex-fiancé), and had her fair share of heartbreak. Much as she wants to meet "the one," tie the knot, and have children, she continually finds herself going from one short-lived relationship to the next. Like clockwork, after three months of dating a man, she manages to find something wrong with him.

Or what about Melanie? A graduate student in California pursuing her Ph.D. in clinical psychology, she longs to find what she calls a "faithful companion," someone who will be there for her through thick and thin. Yet in the past four years, she has dated three men: one with a wife and two children, another who lived outside the country and had no plans to relocate, and a third who was on his way to jail for tax evasion.

And finally, there's Jenna. At 40 years old, she has lived an extremely full life. After breaking off an engagement in her early thirties, she traded her Vera Wang dress for a plane ticket, traveled the world for three months, and eventually started a business serving solo female travelers. She always thought that she would get married at some point in her life, but every time a relationship looked like it was getting serious, she found herself yearning to travel again.

Accustomed to perceiving men as commitment-averse emotional nitwits, all these women point to their former flames' shortcomings as the reasons for why they are still single. Bad luck? Mere coincidence? At what point does one realize that the only common denominator here is the woman herself?

With all this talk about men being commitment-phobic, isn't it high time we looked at ourselves and admit that maybe, just maybe, we are the ones who have become commitment-challenged? Sure, it's easy to point the finger at men, but these days aren't we equally bad when it comes to making a commitment?

Think about it. How many women do you know who claim

that they're dying to commit, only to turn away one potential suitor after another or stay in relationships year after year that offer no hope of commitment? It just doesn't add up. For years, we have been asking the magic question, "What's wrong with him?" And only now are we beginning to think, "Maybe it's me!"

TOP SIGNS YOU'RE COMMITMENT-PHOBIC

If you're ready to finally face the truth about your commitment-phobia, go down the list of these common symptoms and check off the ones that apply.

- Once the excitement of first romance has passed, you get bored in most of your relationships.
- You have a habit of dating unavailable men (married, involved with someone else, geographically or emotionally distant, etc.).
- You have a long and elaborate list of requirements for your ideal mate.
- You go from one short-lived relationship to the next.
- You back out of plans at the last minute and/or have trouble setting a time for dates.
- You often stay in relationships that are rocky and offer little to no hope of commitment.
- You consider your married friends' relationships boring and feel that many of them have settled for too little.
- You tend to feel smothered in a relationship.
- You cultivate larger networks of friends and acquaintances at the expense of single romantic relationships.
- You have a lot of relationship trauma in your past.
- You have a habit of avoiding conversations about marriage and the future with the people you date.
- You date more than one man at a time to prevent becoming dependent.
- You have a tendency to pick fights and criticize your partners.
- You have a difficult time getting over past boyfriends.
- You prefer hook-ups and friends-with-benefits scenarios to relationships.

- Your career is very important to you, and you often choose work over relationships.
- You are constantly blowing hot and cold in your relationships.

CONFESSIONS OF A RECOVERING COMMITMENT-PHOBE

It's time to come clean. I, Elina Furman, have a fear of commitment. I have always been a halfway kind of girl. I usually finish half of what's on my plate before reaching for the dish across from me. I'm halfway through *War and Peace*. And I'm still halfway through planning exotic vacations I'm probably never going to take. The way I look at it, if it's not interesting or engaging halfway through, there's no point in going all the way.

The truth is that I'm terrified of seeing things through. I mean, what if you finish something and then realize it was a colossal waste of time? What if you sign up for a pottery class and find out you're not good at it? Or what if you start painting your bedroom one color and then decide you're not really a lavender person after all? What if you take that vacation only to find out it would have been better left to your imagination? While I'm great at starting and planning, somehow along the way I always lose the motivation to see things through. With so many options and possibilities, it's all too easy to get sidetracked.

So when it comes to relationships, it's no surprise that I was always half committed. Not that I strayed or cheated or anything. In fact, I pride myself on being a great partner. It's just somewhere around the halfway mark, something happens. I lose momentum. I become distracted, depressed, and anxious. I forget why I'm there and start imagining what it would be like to be somewhere else entirely.

The first time I realized I had commitment issues was when my ex-boyfriend of seven years and I broke up. Not that it wasn't devastating, but there was something so anticlimactic about the

Elina Furman

whole thing. Looking back, I remembered a lot of things fondly, but mostly what I remembered was what *didn't* happen.

Besides the fact that it took us four years to even say the word *love*, we had never talked about the future, commitment, marriage, or even living together. In seven long years of dating, the subject never came up—not once. You know how some couples kind of half joke about it or roll their eyes when friends ask, "So when are you two getting married?" Not us. When it came to talking about the serious commitment issues, we never, *ever* discussed, alluded, or even hinted at it.

The thing was, I couldn't imagine *not* having him in my life, but neither could I imagine having him in my life forever. Not permanently, that is. Not until death did us part. As boyfriends went, he was great—caring, fun, supportive, the works! But together forever? At age twenty-five, the one thing I knew for certain was that there wasn't anything I could predict with any certainty. I knew I cared about him, but I also knew there were many men to meet, a gazillion places to be, and a whole lifetime to be lived. I thought, *What if I decide to quit my job, move to the country, and start breeding Maltese puppies? Would I have the option to do that once I was fully committed? Or what if I made the decision to be with him, only to fall in love with someone else?* These questions plagued me on a daily basis.

On the other hand, I was equally scared to leave something good behind. As curious as I was about life's infinite possibilities, I was just as terrified of leaving the safe confines of the relationship. After all, what if this was as good as it got? So there I was: stuck in between—not wanting to lose him but incapable of moving things forward.

Looking back at my life, I realized that I had never really thought about making a commitment to someone. Sure, the concept was always lodged somewhere in the back of my brain, but more like a random afterthought than a concrete idea. It has taken many years of introspection, reviewing my personal history, and watching myself sabotage every good thing in my life to finally realize that as much as I wanted stability and comfort, I was equally if not more petrified of making a permanent commitment.

Whether it was in my halfhearted efforts in school, my half-baked dance career, my quasi-committed relationships, or any of my gazillion half-finished jobs and business ideas, I always found myself losing interest before I could really immerse myself or master something. "Easy come, easy go!" was my motto. And while that attitude gave me the chance to explore a variety of interesting jobs, men, and creative impulses, I realized that in the end I didn't have much to show for myself.

WHY I WROTE THIS BOOK

When I first started pondering this problem, I could have easily dismissed my commitment issues as a simple case of relationship ADD or not having met my "soul mate" (whatever that means). But I knew there was something more to it. I was determined to find out more about my conflicting views on commitment. Call it a hunch, call it women's intuition, but I couldn't help suspecting that there were many other women who experienced the same ambivalence as I did: the conflict of wanting to be with someone but not at the expense of their personal freedom. I was desperate to find out what was at the bottom of these issues, and that's when I set off to find more information to help myself and the many other women struggling with the same problems.

Armed with the best motivations, I scoured the bookstores and libraries hoping to find something that would help me out. Nothing! Not one book about female commitment-phobia. I stopped to wonder: *Can this really be? Am I just imagining all my issues?* But something told me that my anxiety was not merely a figment of my imagination. That's when I set out to find out what was at the root of all this. I had no idea that I was about to embark on what would eventually become an exhilarating, sometimes painful, but mostly eye-opening three-year journey.

My first order of business: reaching out to and interviewing women from all over the country. With every woman I talked to, it was the same story. They wanted commitment but were scared of getting involved. They loved their boyfriends but were terrified of taking the next step. They felt pressure to date but were happier when they were on their own. Dozens of women wrote in, telling me their stories—from the almost-bride who left her husband at the altar and still regrets it to the CEO who has spent her life hiding behind her work because she feared commitment. The e-mails kept pouring in. Some of the women were proud, some were scared, and others were just plain bewildered by their commitment anxiety. No matter what the reaction, all of them shared the same sentiment: "I'm so relieved that there are others like me." The more women I talked to, the more comforted I became as well. I wasn't the only commitment-phobe out there!

WARNING: WHAT THIS BOOK WILL *NOT* DO!

Let's get one thing straight: this book will not help you get married or find the man of your dreams in thirty days or less, nor will it list 365 totally terrific things about being single. I'm not here to convert you, lecture you, or tell you to change your ways. After all, there's no law that says, "Thou shall commit."

This book is not pro-marriage, anti-singles, or couples-obsessed. It is not about convincing you that you need a committed relationship to live a fulfilling life—because you don't. Nor is it about telling you that your life will be perfect if you continue to avoid committed relationships—because it won't.

While many of you will discover that you are shirking commitment due to fears and anxiety, not everyone who chooses to be single is avoiding intimacy. Some women are perfectly happy being on their own, cohabiting, or even having children out of wedlock. There's absolutely nothing wrong with choosing to go it alone if that is in fact what you want to do.

My biggest fear is *not* that you'll spend your life single. No, my greater concern is that you won't stop to examine your underlying beliefs about commitment and will continue to act in ways that are self-defeating and at cross-purposes with your true life goals. The real crisis would be in your failure to understand how your fears and uncertainty drive much of your behavior.

Another thing that you won't find in these pages is someone telling you that you're a victim in love, that you're perpetually "unlucky," or that men are the reasons for all your relationship problems. In fact, one of the main premises of this book is that most of the time you have chosen your love life, whether you know it or not. No matter what you believe, there's no such thing as the "accidental single." Every day, you have made innumerable conscious and unconscious choices that have led up to where you are now. You choose your love life every time you fall for a married man, start dating someone who lives three thousand miles away, or break up a good relationship for no apparent reason.

First and foremost, this book is about committing to yourself, finding inner courage, and honoring your choices—whatever these may be. Throughout this book, when I use the word *commitment*, I won't be referring to getting a giant diamond ring or filing for a marriage certificate. Commitment here means honestly connecting with another person without fear, timidity, or ambivalence. Commitment isn't about getting married. It's about sustaining a lasting and meaningful connection with another human being.

This book will not tell you what you should do with your life, but it will help you become more conscious of your choices so you can start creating a future that's more in line with your goals. If you're happy being on your own or feel that you have no internal blocks that are standing in the way of making a commitment, feel free to use this book as a way to validate your choices. But if you're tired of feeling ambivalent and conflicted about your relationships, this book may just be the commitment cure you've been looking for.

HOW THIS BOOK IS ORGANIZED

If you're reading this book, there's probably a small part of you that thinks you just might be a commitment-phobe. That's why you'll need to find out once and for all. Chapter 2 includes quizzes and exercises to help you figure out if you are indeed afraid of commitment and will show you all the ways in which you may be allowing fear to sabotage your love life.

The second part of the book will help you determine what type of commitment-phobe you are, because when it comes to women, we all know that one size *never* fits all. After countless interviews, I started to recognize several distinct patterns of behavior. While some women serial-dated to avoid committing to one man, others checked out of the dating game altogether as a way of dealing with their relationship anxiety. And still others pursued ambivalent men in order to avoid dealing with their own commitment issues.

Commitment-phobia can manifest itself in a variety of different ways, which is why I have organized the types into seven basic composites: the Nitpicker, Serial Dater, Tinker Bell, Free Spirit, Damsel in Distress, Player, and Long-Distance Runner.

In order to be able to better understand and overcome your issues, it's very important that you take the time to identify your particular type. Each chapter will include hang-ups, potential pitfalls, and concrete steps and strategies personalized for each type of commitment-phobe. You can either review each of the archetypes separately, depending on which you think applies most, or you can read through all of them. Since many commitment-phobes overlap in their behavior, I would highly recommend that you review each one carefully. In fact, I can think of many instances when I've been all of the above types.

Finally, once you've become more aware of your issues, you'll need concrete and practical tools to help you battle your commitment fears. Rest assured, you won't be left high and dry and will find plenty of advice for stopping your commitment-phobia in its tracks. From managing runaway emotions to curbing overanalysis, there are no shortages of practical tools to help you overcome your commitment-phobia once and for all.

READY OR NOT!

With all our gains, benefits, and rising social status, it's no wonder that many of us women are becoming more commitment-phobic. While living alone and cultivating ourselves is an important rite of passage, many of us are getting stuck in this phase. We become so comfortable with the single life that we become scared to take the emotional risks a committed relationship requires.

There are numerous ways in which we avoid commitment—whether we do things halfway, reject people we care about, conceal our true feelings, or keep one foot out the door at all times to protect ourselves. Looking back on my life, I realize that the fear of seeing something through and committing myself wholeheartedly was more about my fear of failure than anything else, because if I didn't put all of myself into something, then I couldn't be blamed when it didn't work out. And that, of course, was a guarantee that nothing ever did.

In the end, there is only one surefire way to forge a solid relationship, and that's to be ready for one. It's not enough to claim to *want* a relationship. You have to be emotionally ready to commit. And that's the ultimate goal here: to help you ready yourself for commitment so that when love comes knocking on your door, you won't slam it shut.

1

She's Got Issues

Whether you're dragging your Manolos down the aisle, rejecting every available man in your zip code, or jumping ship every time a man brings up the future, many of you are right now suffering from commitment-phobia. As novel as the concept may seem, it's hardly a laughing matter. I mean, how funny is it to want something, drive yourself crazy fantasizing about it every day, and then when you finally get it, drop it like last year's Ugg boots? I don't know about you, but there's something downright unnerving about being so conflicted—about thinking you want the whole enchilada (marriage, kids, live-in boyfriend, or husband) and when the time comes to sign on some dotted line (be it a one-year lease or a marriage certificate) realizing that you don't. Not even close. Not at all. Well, maybe a little.

THE CONFESSIONAL: Jane, 38

It's weird—now that I turned 38, I'm much calmer about the whole thing. But that wasn't always the case. For fifteen years, I spent all my time looking, dating, and trying to find Mr. Right. I read every self-help book. I visited psychologists, tarot readers, psychics—you name it, I did it. During those years, I met some great people, but nothing ever worked out. I remember all the heartache, the drama, the feeling that I just had to find someone or die trying, all the classes I took and all the insecurities I had, like maybe I was unlovable. I finally met someone a year ago. He was everything I thought I wanted—good-looking, stable, nice, secure, funny. And then out of nowhere, I freaked out and broke

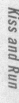

> up with him. It was a huge shock to realize that I actually missed being single. Everyone thought I was crazy. But I know I'm not half as crazy as I used to be. At least, now I know what I want. I can't help regretting all that time I spent agonizing over my relationships and worrying about being alone. I wish I would have figured it out sooner and enjoyed those years a little more. I don't know . . . hobbies, traveling more, whatever—just focusing on my needs instead of running around town like some crazy woman.

For years, I have watched many women struggle with commitment anxiety. I have seen perfectly sane females insist that their one goal in life is to have a stable relationship, and then do everything in their power to avoid it. Or those women who go on ad infinitum about their careers, the joys of living solo, and no-strings sex, only to collapse in a weeping heap when a guy doesn't call when he says he will. And how could we forget those who are so terrified of facing their commitment fears that they break up with someone they love when things get too close?

Let's face it—many of us can't even commit to a hair color, let alone a full-fledged, long-term relationship. And it's not just your typical runaway-bride scenario, either. You don't have to have a gaggle of bridesmaids and a reception hall reservation to experience cold feet. In fact, there are a million and one ways we express our fear of commitment, whether it's by staying in go-nowhere relationships, cheating on our spouses, blowing up our boyfriends' tiny flaws to mammoth proportions, serial dating, or hiding out at home watching reruns of *Sex and the City*. The behaviors may vary, but the underlying cause is the same: *we want to engage in long-term committed relationships but are terrified of what we'll have to give up in the process.*

Whether you recognize yourself or any of your single girl-friends in any of the above scenarios, you have to admit one thing: our commitment issues are starting to get a little out of hand. With so many options and conflicting messages (Date! Don't date! Be independent! Find someone to love!), it's no surprise that women are acting just a wee bit schizophrenic. Stuck in a seemingly endless cycle of desire, ambivalence, and confusion, many single women simply don't know that they are afraid of the very things they think they want—commitment and stability.

YOU'RE SO NOT ALONE

As millions of single women stand on the threshold of commitment, struggling with their fears as they try to decide whether to get married, cohabit, or break up, many of them wonder:

- Is this normal?
- Why am I feeling so anxious?
- Am I the only one who feels this way?

The answers to these questions are simple: (1) Yes, it's normal. (2) Because commitment is scary. (3) And no, you're not alone.

The Census Bureau reports that single women are the fastest-growing segment of the American population, with more than 47 million in this country, 22 million of whom fall within the 25-to-44 age range. Many of these women are right now struggling with commitment anxiety.

While it's becoming clear that women have immense anxiety about commitment and are pushing back marriage later every year, there is almost no information about our ambivalence. As a result, many of us feel completely alone when in fact there are millions of others just like us. The most important thing to realize is that you're not alone. Not even close!

CPs Around the World

If you thought American women had major commitment issues, you'd be surprised to find that your girlfriends around the globe are just as stumped. Here's how some other countries stack up in the commitment department.

Kiss and Run

13

United States: The number of women living alone has increased more than 33 percent in the past fifteen years to 30 million, and the marriage rate in 2004 has declined nearly 50 percent since 1970, from 76.5 marriages per 1,000 unmarried women to 39.9 *(State of Our Union, National Marriage Project).*

Japan: The number of unmarried Japanese women ages 25 to 34 is skyrocketing, so much so that the government is enacting policies to ensure the continuation of the population. How apocalyptic! What used to be a very family-centric culture has quickly become single-minded, with a bestseller about life as a thirty-something single female, titled *Howl of the Loser Dogs,* flying off the shelves and Boyfriend Pillows (headrests shaped like a man's arm) selling out as quickly as they're made.

Brits: When it comes to our friends across the pond, they're taking commitment-phobia to a whole new level. With the average age of women getting married now at 32 years (Office of National Statistics, 2001), there's a reason why singleton Bridget Jones was invented here. And with a new National Singles Week holiday to call their very own, it's unlikely that the trend will reverse anytime soon.

Aussies: Australia's marriage rate is the lowest it has been in a hundred years. Nearly a third of all Australian women from 30 to 34 are single. And this from the people who brought us *Muriel's Wedding?*

NOT YOUR MOTHER'S PROBLEM

Female commitment-phobia is a relatively new phenomenon. Not to say that our mothers didn't struggle with a certain amount of anxiety, because they did, and many still do. But when it came to 'fessing up to their commitment issues, the old-girl network never stood a chance. Back then, the idea of an unmarried girl on the loose was just plain unheard of. In fact, they had another, not-so-flattering name for that type of girl.

When it came right down to it, there just wasn't any room for ambiguity or indecision. Like it or not, a woman had to maintain a certain measure of semi-respectability. Translation: get married and have kids, pronto! Those who struggled with committing usually stayed silent, sucked it up, and went through with it despite their misgivings. Our mothers just didn't have the wherewithal to defy these expectations (ever see those pouty bride photos from the old days?). Besides those awful cone-shaped bras, there was a good reason why so many of them looked so peevish.

Of course, there were a few rare exceptions. Not everyone walked gently into that good night of matrimonial bliss. There were the brazen sex-kitten screen stars such as Mae West, fiercely independent actresses like Katharine Hepburn, and unrepentant serial wedders Elizabeth Taylor and Hedy Lamarr. These feisty femmes were around kicking up a storm the whole time, but no one really noticed or cared to think about the matter much. After all, they were famous, and certain allowances had to be made for Hollywood types.

But that was then. And now? Well, we have a much bigger problem on our hands. We're still confronted with a barrage of social pressure to settle down and commit, but it's not like anyone really cares what we do anymore (save for dear old Grammy and De Beers, of course). These days women are free to choose rather than just be influenced by social pressure. We have more opportunities than ever before. We can get married, get divorced, travel the world, run a Fortune 500 company, play the field, cohabit, have kids, adopt puppies, all of the above, or none of it. It's really anyone's call.

THE CONFESSIONAL: Avery, 25

I think that women's commitment-phobia stems from not wanting to settle for something right now, especially since something better might come along. We've seen our mothers and grandmothers who did settle and are unhappy because of it. I think that one advantage of staying single is that you control your own destiny. You aren't tied to someone else who could potentially bring you down. My mother was a housewife

> *for most of my childhood. I'm afraid of being trapped in a situation where I am just a wife/mother and feeling as though my potential is untapped. I also feel like this time in my life is about being selfish—growing up and developing myself. If I'm not selfish now, I don't want to have a midlife crisis and be selfish later when the stakes are higher.*

So what exactly is the problem? you're wondering. Before you start burning your bras and celebrating in the name of female empowerment, consider that we might have gotten more than we bargained for. With all our talk about winning the right to choose, that's exactly where the problem lies: choice and more choices! With all the emphasis on the *right* to choose, there's been little talk of *how* to choose.

The truth is many of us grew up thinking that we would one day be picked, rather than having to do the picking ourselves. Schooled in the art of capturing a man, flirting, and looking good, we never learned how to scrutinize, analyze, and evaluate the opposite sex. It was enough that he fit a standard ideal of the "right" guy—financially secure, polite, and color-coordinated. We may have the power to make our own decisions now, but that doesn't mean we're any more equipped than our mothers to make good ones.

With so many dizzying options to pick from, today's women are far more prone to catching the commitment-phobia bug than ever before. Think about it. It's all too easy to decide on a coat of paint for your bedroom when you only have a choice of two colors. But when presented with a rainbow of equally pleasing options (caramel latte, polo blue, acorn yellow), the whole matter can become far more confusing than it needs to be. And when it comes to making a decision about love, the rest of your life, or even the next few years, it's all too easy to freak out and lose our heads. With choice comes responsibility, and that's the hardest pill of all to swallow.

If you think our mothers had it rough in that department, consider that their lack of opportunities could have been a blessing in disguise. Not that I'm proposing to go back to the old regime or anything. After all, many of our mothers are now left with the hard work of reinventing themselves after never having the opportunity to invent themselves properly in the first place. But you have to admit that life seemed a little bit easier back then. So before you start thinking about how much luckier you are than dear old Mom, stop to consider that our freedom exacts its own price, and its name is commitment-phobia. While your mom may wonder what it is like to be in your shoes every now and then, rest assured she's also pretty damn glad she isn't.

THE TIMES ARE A-CHANGIN'

No matter what you call it—commitment-phobia, cold feet, run-away-bride syndrome—the results are the same: a new breed of women with an enormous sense of entitlement, unwilling to put up with less-than-perfect behavior, poor style choices, or person-ality flaws. With so many factors contributing to this phenome-non, let's stop to consider what's really behind our newfound reluctance to commit.

THE DOCTOR IS IN

I think that women are freer to make their own decisions than they were 150 years ago. In light of the women's movement, women are ex-pressing themselves in a larger way because they can. They actually do have a voice. I think their independence can become an issue, making women a little more selective, potentially. I think women of old used to settle more. That's why I think it's more of a phenomenon today.
—*Dr. Michael S. Broder*

1. Money Honeys

It used to be that the marital institution guaranteed an upgrade in lifestyle and social status. In the eighteenth and nineteenth centuries, remaining single was often tantamount to a lifetime of menial labor and penury: women would be turned out of their parents' houses, forced to work in demeaning occupations, and sometimes even starve due to a lack of marital opportunities. So when the first man came along who could rescue them from their squalid conditions, you can bet that they didn't spend time ticking off all his annoying habits or raising hell when he picked the wrong restaurant. They were just glad to have something to eat.

But all that's changed. The American way has always been about the quest for something better—a bigger dream, a better house, a higher-paying job. And with women finally getting a bigger share of the economic pie, it's become the woman's way as well. Judging by such *Newsweek* cover headlines as "She Works, He Doesn't: The Latest Twist in Jobs and Family (Why 30% of Working Women Make More than Their Husbands)," it's obvious that women are making considerable economic strides.

Despite the fact that women still earn 78 cents for every dollar a man makes, we've certainly come a long way. A 2003 National Association of Realtors survey found that 21 percent of home purchases were made by single women and that they are fast on their way to becoming the most active buyers in the market, even outpacing single men. What's more, single women in the United States account for 50 percent of stock market investing. Entrepreneurially speaking, we're also leading the pack by owning more than 35 percent of U.S. companies and employing more than 27 million people.

With money and social status ceasing to be a primary factor in the choice of partner, it's clear that women's growing financial independence has lessened the urgency to commit. No longer dependent on men for financial security and social status, women are reveling in their freedom and are worried that making a commitment would mean renouncing all that they have worked so hard to attain. So with work and men both vying for equal attention, something usually has to give. And for the professional modern woman, that something is usually romantic relationships.

THE CONFESSIONAL: Gloria, 38

My career is very important to me. I need to feel purposeful and that I'm constantly growing and learning. As a result, I often choose work over relationships. My mother, because of a bad marriage, had to give up a lucrative job. She's always felt unfulfilled, and in some respects, I believe that she resents us (my dad, my siblings) for keeping her from realizing her goals. And I see my sister, who needs to be Suzy Homemaker to make her husband happy. I feel like her identity is totally wrapped up in her status as a wife and soon-to-be mother. I don't want that to happen to me. At the end of the day, you can point to your achievements and say, "That's mine and no one else's." That's important to me. I worry that I would be less inclined to take opportunities because of my partner.

2. *Le Divorce:* Unhappily Ever After

If our careers are a convenient excuse to avoid commitment, then the collective fear of divorce is an even bigger doozy. I mean, who would be brave enough to get in a car if it meant you had a 50 percent chance of dying before you got where you were going? Talk about some bad odds!

Having lived through the record-setting divorce decade of the 1980s, many of us have developed a natural suspicion of the marital institution. Because our parents were expected to get married, have kids, and put everything else on hold (many times before they were sufficiently ready), disillusion, dismay, and divorce frequently followed. As a result, many of us are understandably gun-shy, having seen the devastating effects that divorce can have. Even if our parents gallantly stuck it out for the sake of the children, putting up with the constant turmoil in our younger years often made us wish they hadn't.

Whether it was watching our parents quarrel, toil away in unfulfilling relationships, or suffer the hardships that accompany a single-parent lifestyle, we swore that that would never be us; we vowed to never end up in a similar situation. Now that we're older and, we hope, a bit wiser, many of us still haven't quite gotten over the past.

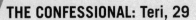

THE CONFESSIONAL: Teri, 29

My parents are divorced. My dad is remarried to a woman eighteen years his junior and is a workaholic, and my mom is single and dating. My mom tends to date guys with a lot of money and older or much younger. I take marriage really seriously. I have seen too many people look at it like, "Well, you can always get a divorce, so what the heck." I think it would work for me because I am not one to settle for just anyone I am comfortable with, and I am realistic on the downsides because I have seen it all before.

With the 50 percent marital survival rate lodged firmly in our brains, there's a lot more riding on our choices. The stakes of love become so high that it becomes virtually impossible to relate to others in a calm and nonvigilant manner. We worry that the wrong choice of partner could lead to an unhappy union, culminating in an acrimonious and bitter divorce.

If he even as much as glances at another girl, we mentally file him away as a serial cheater. If he innocently asks us to do the dishes one night, we imagine a life of household chores and domestic drudgery. If he doesn't call three nights in a row, we brand him a raging commitment-phobe, thus conveniently avoiding dealing with our own anxiety about commitment. And his socks, the ones that looked so cute lying on the living room floor when we first started dating, suddenly morph into deal breakers once he's moved in.

With so many failed marriages, soured relationships, and broken unions, many of us assume that in order to be successful in love, we have to beat the system and find the one person who is perfect for us in every way, the one person who will never, ever land us in divorce court. But as we all know, there's no such thing as a divorce insurance policy.

THE DOCTOR IS IN

Parents who got divorced can have a very big impact on women in terms of fear of commitment, especially if it was a volatile divorce or if

Elina Furman

20

3. Thirty Going on 13

Is 30 really the new 20? We've all heard that one before. But there's definitely more than a little truth to that statement. Our world is undergoing a radical shift in its expectations of when we mature. The MacArthur Foundation's Transition to Adulthood project has set a new ceiling for adolescence at 34 years of age. And the 2005 U.S. Census Bureau's marriage statistics indicate that women are waiting longer than ever to settle down, with the average age of first marriage increasing from 20.8 to 25.8 between 1970 and 2005. Just as we've all heard about the Peter Pan complex, the boy who wouldn't grow up, it was only a matter of time before the Tinker Bell Syndrome reared its head.

THE DOCTOR IS IN

The whole social expectation of mating is a sign of maturity, leading to the mythical 2.5 children, the dog, and the white picket fence. This is the cultural expectation of what you do when you grow up. And so just as men are affected by what's been called the Peter Pan Syndrome, women, too, can see that their parents or other grown-ups are not having as much fun in their lives and it doesn't look very attractive. And it's easy for them to say, "I don't want to go there." We don't really have rites of passage in our culture anymore. And in the absence of other rites of passage, marriage has become the main symbol of being grown up.

—*Dr. Deborah Anapol*

In the past, our youth was defined as a time of personal struggle for identity that ended with the choice of a career and a spouse. These were the goalposts on the road to adulthood. Whether it's because of our extended life span (77.6 years in 2003) or the fact that it's taking far longer to match our parents' middle-class lifestyle, we don't feel as compelled to get a job, settle down, and push out 2.5 kids all before we turn 30. In fact, more and more studies are encouraging women to wait, showing that late marriages have better success rates than early ones.

What used to be the years for moving to the suburbs and picking out china patterns have now become a time of unabashed self-exploration, a period to experiment, travel, date, establish a career, and nurture social networks. Having postponed marriage and carved out a thriving single life for ourselves, many of us have become habituated to living on our own, much like a confirmed bachelor. In the end, today's women are in no hurry to grow up, and it is these new expectations for the onset of adulthood that have eliminated the urgency with which many of us pursue commitment.

THE CONFESSIONAL: Lia, 33

I have a huge fear of aging and death, and view marriage as a milestone followed by a series of losses. I see people around me finding happiness and peace within scenarios that on paper look entirely unriveting. It makes me wonder if there is something to be said for boring. Then again, the idea of being saddled with a husband and children right now is terrifying. I think I just move at a slower pace than some of my peers.

4. Hip to Be Single

Fifty years ago, a single woman who postponed marriage would have been branded a spinster, an old maid, or a recluse. Unwed women were usually derided, barely tolerated, or viewed as home-wrecking threats. Thankfully, today's social climate has changed drastically.

Look around and you'll see images of the hip single woman everywhere. There's the immense popularity of the chick-lit genre, national singles organizations, TV shows such as *Sex and the City*, singles registries at stores such as Williams-Sonoma and Pottery Barn, and diamond companies marketing right-hand rings to celebrate women's independence. Sure, there are the occasional eyebrow furrows when you tell someone you're single, but overall the stigma of being uncoupled has dramatically decreased, helping women shake off the spinster stereotype and celebrate their single years.

But can it really be all that simple? Not at all. In fact, life has become more complicated than ever. On one hand, it is perfectly acceptable for us to enjoy a variety of relationships without long-term commitment. On the other hand, many of us still have traditional leanings and crave stability, family, and commitment.

5. Mommy Madness

Single mothers may have made for startling headlines in the past, but today they're old news. The idea of a woman having or adopting a kid by herself doesn't even faze us anymore. But life hasn't always been this sweet for the single mommy. Besides the lack of financial opportunity, a woman in the past who wanted to have children either had to get married or face a meager existence on the fringes of society. Not only that, she would have to risk her children being ostracized as well.

Fortunately, the stigma of having kids outside the confines of a conventional marriage scenario has significantly decreased. A record number of babies (almost 1.5 million) were born to unmarried women in the United States in 2004. And according to new data from the Federal National Center for Health Statistics, those mothers were much more likely to be in their twenties than to be teenage moms. It's obvious that women who want kids today find that they don't have to wait around for their knight in shining armor to enjoy the benefits of motherhood.

But the issue of single mommies isn't quite so cut-and-dried. Some women struggle with the idea of going it alone and wouldn't dream of having children outside of marriage. For these women, their ticking biological clocks are a constant reminder that they have yet to make a commitment. Many of them are legitimately freaked out that their fear of permanency will impede their chances of starting a family. With nine times more fertility clinics in the United States now than there were in 1986, it should come as no surprise that women are delaying having children well into their thirties and forties. And yet, there are many women who are as averse to the idea of having children as to the prospect of committing to a relationship. For them, committing to a child or a man poses an equal-opportunity challenge of giving up the freedom and mobility that they currently enjoy.

THE CONFESSIONAL: Casey, 28

I definitely think about getting older. My mother said she went to this wedding last night and the bride was 30 and we were talking how she should be having babies. And my mom said, "Yeah, she's up there." And I'm like, "What do you mean? I'm knocking on 30." You do have to think about marriage and babies—age definitely affects what you look for when you are going to be dating someone. But it also scares me, because I think, if I find that person, am I really going to want to be with them for the rest of my life? And marriage usually leads to children, and that's the other extreme where you are not only responsible for yourself, but you are responsible for this other life. That changes the whole dynamic of your life. Everyone speaks about how wonderful it is, and that it's a love you will never experience anywhere else. But you can't know that until it actually happens. And it takes away a lot of your freedom and your identity. You have to be really selfless.

6. Chick Cliques

In lieu of committed relationships, many women are forming close-knit groups that serve as surrogate support networks. You can't walk by a bar or restaurant without seeing a group of women toasting their friendships and successes. And who could forget all those hours you and your friends clock on the phone or at your

Elina Furman

regular Sunday brunches? The idea now seems to be, "Who needs a boyfriend when I have so many friends?" Women can travel together, start businesses together, live together, and support each other during a health scare or crisis.

THE CONFESSIONAL: Danielle, 31

I have a ton of friends—I'm a very social person, I get along with people really well. I just think someone who will be sharing that part of me will have to be not just someone that I trust, but someone who is—not like a hero, but bigger than me. I don't want to sound all Sex and the City (I think that was a line on the show), but I'd rather be alone than be with the wrong person. I'd rather spend time with friends.

With many of their social and personal needs being met by friends, it's no surprise that women are more likely to question commitment. Some of these surrogate urban tribes are so emotionally supportive and rewarding that women do not feel the need to form traditional nuclear families of their own. In the absence of one significant other, many women find themselves turning to their friends for support.

Of course, what starts out as a great substitute often becomes a convenient way to push away commitment. After all, who has time to commit to a long-term relationship when life is already so full? Suddenly, men are finding that they have to jump through hoops to pry a woman away from her friends or worry that they will be disqualified if they fail to impress her girlfriends.

CINE-PHOBIA: COMMITMENT-PHOBIA IN THE MOVIES

No matter how perplexing our issues are in real life, female commitment-phobes are riveting to watch on the big screen. Here are a few of the most memorable.

Runaway Bride (1999): Who could forget the classic image of Julia Roberts racing away from the altar on horseback? In the movie, the phenomenon of a woman who won't commit is so shocking to the world at large that a famous New York reporter, played by Richard Gere, must fly into her small town to prove the existence of this strange creature. Can this really be true? Can such a woman really exist?

Breakfast at Tiffany's (1961): It's ironic that a movie about a commitment-challenged girl-about-town would serve as the inspirational theme for so many weddings. The film introduces us to Holly Golightly, a madcap single gal who sips champagne before breakfast and survives on her wiles and megawatt charm. To her, money equals freedom, and the word *love* is not in her vocabulary. Until, that is, she meets a man who helps her realize that her fear of being captured is a trap in itself because she cannot truly ever love anyone. While the film intimates that Holly may have finally met her true match, Truman Capote's original book, on which the film was loosely based, has Holly fleeing to Brazil, never to be heard from again. In the end, Holly became an emblem for single women who refused to play by anyone's rules but their own.

Bridget Jones's Diary (2001): Bridget Jones, played expertly by Renée Zellweger, has become the modern symbol of the liberated if slightly neurotic (okay, more than slightly neurotic) single woman. While so many critics and reviewers pegged the lead character as a woman desperate for commitment, Bridget Jones is the ultimate commitment-phobic female, torn between having fun with bad boy Daniel Cleaver (Hugh Grant) and settling down with the stable and serious Mark Darcy (Colin Firth). We should all be so lucky to have her problems. Despite the fact that she frets about being alone, so much of her behavior is self-sabotaging. She continues to engage in a fantasy relationship with the roguish Daniel and constantly picks on poor Mark for being dull and boring. It took a second book/movie and the threat of a life sentence in a Thai prison for her to finally reconcile herself to the notion of long-term commitment.

The Graduate (1967): Even though it was made more than thirty years ago, *The Graduate* stands the test of time as one of the greatest movies ever made about the fear of commitment. What's unique about this film is that it shows both a man and a woman struggling equally with the same issues. When Dustin Hoffman crashes Katherine Ross's wedding to the "wrong" man, the audience cheers him on. Now the couple can make a commitment to each other and live happily ever after. When the bus whisks them away, their smiles slowly fade as they face the realization that they're nowhere near ready to make a lifelong pact.

THE CONFESSIONAL: Kira, 41

I think women can definitely be commitment-phobic. I think the general difference is that it's not as obvious that we are commitment-phobic because it's not a stereotype of women to be that way. Many men just take it as the woman is cold or not into him at all, so men will just give up. On the contrary, when a man is commitment-phobic, the woman will just keep trying because it's a stereotype for men to be that way and she may think she can change him or that he is just a typical man. I think it would be great if more people knew about this problem so that guys would become more aware and consider that this may be the reason why I act the way I do instead of that I am just not interested. That way, men could learn to give me a little space and understand, especially while I am trying to understand myself!!

NOT YOUR BOYFRIEND'S PROBLEM

The stereotype of the elusive bachelor is everywhere. You know, those lads who never make plans until the last minute, date three women at a time, and are always bragging about dodging the marriage bullet. Society just loves to pigeonhole men and women into these Mars/Venus categories. Men are commitment-phobes and women are commitment-holics. End of discussion. Or is it?

In the past, women were brought up to play with dolls, plan their weddings, and imagine their knight in shining armor long before they even learned to finger-paint. In many cases, it *was* the woman who dragged the man across the marital threshold. Men would mumble about being caught hook, line, and sinker, and women would be congratulated on landing such a fine catch.

Despite evidence to the contrary and more and more women choosing to stay single, many of the old stereotypes persist. Everywhere you look, it's still one variation on this theme after another. Whether it's a businesslike plan to nab the love of your life or a time-tested formula for getting him to propose, women are constantly being taught that it's somehow their responsibility to find a man and get him to commit.

But a recent CBS/*New York Times* poll of teenagers produced some startling results that defy many of these gender-alizations. The survey found that boys had much more traditional ideas about marriage and family than the girls. According to this study, "The girls surveyed were more likely than the boys to say they could have a happy life even if they do not marry and that they would consider becoming a single parent." Only 61 percent of the boys thought they could be happy if they didn't get married, while 73 percent of the girls said they could live a happy life without getting married.

In the end, there's no use placing blame on the powers that be. The stereotypes are just as much our fault as anyone's. After all, we girls have enabled the notion of the commitment-phobic man and commitment-hungry woman. We believed it when they told us, "He's just not that into you," and never stopped to wonder if in fact we're into him, committed relationships, and all that they entail.

The fact is, fear of commitment is an equal-opportunity relationship killer. The view of this phobia as a strictly male issue has led us to turn a blind eye to the effect it has on us, and it's high time we realized that we are just as responsible for our love lives and start figuring out what, if anything, we want to do about it. So while pointing the finger at men may make us feel wonderfully neurosis-free, it doesn't help us come to grips with the underlying causes of our fear.

THE GENDERLESS DIVIDE

In the battle of the sexes, even commitment-phobia is up for grabs. Many of you are probably trying to figure out who's more phobic, men or women. So if you're wondering how the genders really compare in the commitment-phobia department, read on to find out.

1. Time's Ticking

Tick. Tock. It's been said that no matter how commitment-phobic or independent a woman is, she will probably want to settle down once her biological clock starts ticking. And while it's true that our chances of conceiving drop at 35, it's important to note that men aren't exactly off the hook here, either. According to *The Male Biological Clock: The Startling News About Aging, Sexuality, and Fertility in Men* by Harry Fisch, M.D., men older than 35 are twice as likely to be infertile as men who are 25. So whether they know it or not, it seems that men are now in the same fertility boat. But does that mean that every guy will automatically jump into commitment mode once he reaches the ripe old age of 35? Highly doubtful. Because despite biology and the urgings of our reproductive systems, many men and women are simply not ready to say goodbye to the single life. In the end, just because our eggs are ready to get hatched doesn't mean we're emotionally ready to get hitched.

2. Nature or Nurture?

We women are often credited with having innate nurturing instincts. Men were the hunters and gatherers, while women held down the fort and protected the little ones. Not to go against years of social conditioning, but the roles aren't as clearly defined as they used to be. Getting food is as easy as calling a reservation hotline, and what with twenty-four-hour convenience stores and all, women are plenty adept at hunting and gathering their own supplies. Also, with so many women spending their time in corporate boardrooms, many have put a premium on developing male-specific traits such as competition and aggression at the expense of female-centric traits such as cooperation and empathy.

Despite the popular wisdom that all women are able to emote and nurture till the cows come home, many of us never learned to share feelings, act selflessly, cooperate, and make the kind of compromises that relationships require. Most of us can't even bring ourselves to hand over the remote control, let alone the reins to our future happiness. In fact, in a poll conducted by Women Today Online, half of the women surveyed said they didn't see themselves as nurturing in a way that comes naturally to them. In the end, for all that talk about us women being born more emotionally intuitive, the shifting economic tides and our newfound career focus have made us no more emotionally wise than men in the realm of personal relationships.

THE CONFESSIONAL: Julie, 36

I'm not really into having kids. I think I'd rather have nice, fabulous affairs. I don't think marriage is the ultimate goal of anything. I have a brother, and I think that's his goal—he wants to fall in love and find somebody and have kids. He once asked me for a nephew for Christmas, and I looked at him like he was insane.

3. Why Buy the Cow When You Can Order a Quart of Milk Online?

In the past, women who wanted to move in with a boyfriend would get a strict talking-to about a common male mentality: "Why buy the cow when you can get the milk for free?" It's often been said that men are postponing marriage because they can now have all the sex they want without any of the emotional commitment. After all, why get married if you can have all the conjugal benefits without any of the fuss? Seems like a tempting enough proposition. Of course, that argument supposes that women don't enjoy sex for its own sake but instead have to use it as a lure to make a man settle down. Problem is, sex is no longer the commitment bait it used to be. Today, both women and men are finding that they don't need to settle down to have sex and can experiment with a variety of partners, which often results in both genders experiencing a host of commitment issues.

It used to be that a woman who had sex outside of marriage was considered loose and immoral. Today, that notion has gone out the window. Plenty of women are having no-strings sex and enjoying every minute of it (more on that later in "The Player" chapter). Women are just as enticed by the prospect of casual sex and (except for a small percentage) don't see anything wrong with a few carnal marathons before marriage.

So while men may still have a slightly higher propensity to enjoy no-strings sex (due to the waning but still powerful double standard), it doesn't mean that men do not yearn for committed relationships or that women have no sexual desires beyond lifelong monogamy. In fact, a study by a university showed that there is no statistical difference between the genders' desires for stable relationships. The 2005 Bowdoin Student Life Survey found that 66 percent of men and 61 percent of women want to be in a relationship (and this from college students at their sexual prime).

THE CONFESSIONAL: Melissa, 24

I don't want to be with anybody seriously right now. I really like being by myself. I really like just having my own voice in my head. Not having it mediated by someone else's opinion. I think I would have to be more fully formed, more strongly formed, before I can be in a committed relationship. I feel like I could be guided into a lifestyle that's not quite right for me and into a way of thinking that doesn't suit me. And it could really close me off from growing in the way that I need to grow. And I get a lot more out of random experiences. I don't want to get tied up with someone. I think it's important to think about your own goals and not to think about what other people want for you.

4. A Sharper Image

It's not surprising that men are growing more conscious of women's commitment-phobia. Nowhere is this more evident than in the trend of "metrosexual men." You know, that color-coordinated guy at your office with the Valentino suit and moisturized skin who you thought was gay until he showed up at the office party with a lingerie model. Since most adults today, ages 18 to 59, can expect to spend around nineteen years living alone (according to *The Sexual Organization of the City* report), men are quickly realizing that their bachelorhood is not necessarily a temporary arrangement. Many have discovered that if they want to have any hope of living in a civilized and organized manner, they must learn to take care of themselves.

With so many women achieving success in the workplace and leading full, active lives, men are also finding that they have to step up their game in order to set themselves apart in the dating market. The pressure to maintain appearances and succeed in a competitive dating atmosphere is certainly intense. Consider the fact that more men are getting plastic surgery that ever, with over 1.2 million procedures performed in 2004, according to the American Society for Aesthetic Plastic Surgery.

It's no longer enough to just bring home the bacon; today's man needs to cook it, serve it, and even garnish it. The more women advance, the higher their standards become for their partners. As a result, many women will no longer accept men who expect them to keep the house clean, take care of the children, *and* go to a full-time job every morning. So whether it's through watching shows such as *Queer Eye for the Straight Guy*, taking cooking classes, or getting facials at the spa, men are finding that they have to improve their overall lifestyles in order to attract today's modern woman.

THE DOCTOR IS IN

In general, I think men and women are more similar than we want to recognize. Of course, there are differences. One of the big differences in the way the fear of commitment shows up is that for the man, it's more expected that he be afraid of commitment. It's more likely that it comes out directly with a man. With a woman, she's not expected to be afraid of commitment, so it may come out a little sideways. A woman might say, "I would commit if I found the right man." Rather than taking the responsibility and saying, "I don't want a partner," it's very convenient for her to find there's no man who's good enough.

—*Dr. Deborah Anapol*

The evidence is clear: when it comes to commitment, both women and men suffer equally. The only difference between male and female anxiety is that men aren't afraid to admit to it. After all, it's all too easy for them. There's the notion that bachelors are Lotharios fending off women right and left. As a result, most men are actually proud of their commitment-shy status, since it bestows on them a certain unattainable allure.

But when it comes to women, singleness is considered not an asset but a liability. Despite the gradual shift, women who are single are still assumed to have been left on the shelf too long or have three legs. As Bridget Jones so aptly described the single set, "It doesn't help that underneath our clothes our entire bodies are covered in scales." Our culture sends so many mixed messages about singlehood, spinsterhood, and our "duty" to settle down that we don't quite know what to make of all our conflicting emotions and ambivalence. So while some women do own up to their commitment issues, most will try to deny them for as long as possible, thinking that it will make them seem abnormal, strange, and somehow unfeminine.

WHAT'S LOVE GOT TO DO WITH IT?

Poetry, religion, literature, philosophy . . . since the beginning of time, all have exalted the transcendent power that love has over the human soul. So it's no surprise that within the heart of even most vehement commitment-phobes lies the need to love and be loved.

So with all this talk about pursuing careers, the perfect man, and personal growth, one has to wonder what many of us women are giving up. By ignoring our desire for stable and loving unions, we are actually turning down the very thing that will ultimately give purpose and meaning to our lives. By avoiding commitment and stable relationships, aren't we actually committing to another course . . . often without even realizing it?

In our bid for equality and personal freedom, many of us have sorely neglected our fundamentally human need for love and sharing. Despite our best efforts at independence, most of us still long for the companionship, comfort, and connection of a solid, committed relationship. We know we don't need a man, but therein lies the whole problem: *we have become so emancipated that we are shutting out real love from our lives.*

Instead of working to live, we live to work. Instead of opening up, we build insurmountable walls. Instead of learning to share, we become more guarded. Many of us have come to view men as either deterrents to our happiness or harmless distractions, and we have become less capable of relating to them in a meaningful way. And while no one would argue that committed relationships don't require some degree of compromise, the price we pay for avoiding them entirely can be much dearer still.

So whether you're tired of acting unavailable, constantly falling in love with unsuitable men, or feeling terrified of taking your relationship to the next level, it's high time you got into the driver's seat and on the road to facing down your commitment fears once and for all.

2

So Are You or Aren't You?

When the idea of male commitment-phobia was first introduced by Steven Carter in the book *Men Who Can't Love*, it was a revolutionary concept. Today, we can't go five minutes without branding some poor unsuspecting guy a raging commitment-phobe. Well, the same thing is now happening to women. In the past, it may have seemed crazy to suggest that women could be commitment-phobic, but just because female commitment-phobia isn't common knowledge or studied in psychological journals, that doesn't mean that millions aren't suffering from the anxiety at this very minute. I've done extensive research and conducted numerous interviews with psychologists and with women out in the dating world, and it's clear that female commitment-phobia is alive, well, and far more common than many of us realize.

While this condition may not be obvious to the rest of the world, what is painfully obvious is that many of you will have a hard time coming to terms with this diagnosis. There's no denying it's a touchy subject. To be honest, I have yet to meet a woman (or man, for that matter) who did not have some kind of emotional reaction to this topic. Many of you simply don't want to think that your relationship issues have to do with your own ambivalence. Not that I could blame you. It's easier to blame the fates, bad luck, or your parents than admit you might have some issues committing.

THE DOCTOR IS IN

Figuring out if you are commitment-phobic is really a scary thing to do because women in our culture are all raised to think that we want rela-

So if you find yourself crying, shouting, or rejoicing at the news of this discovery, rest assured that if you have any of the follow reactions (collected from personal interviews) you're in good company.

1. **Denial.** "I couldn't possibly have commitment-phobia. I'm totally open to the prospect of meeting someone. Nope, that's not me. I'm always on the lookout for a new relationship. It just never works out. It's really the men's fault. I just can't seem to find anyone to settle down with, except that one guy, hmmm . . . No, he was really just a little too nice. I don't think it would have worked out."

2. **Pride.** "Hell, yeah! I love my commitment-phobia. It's like my best friend. It's amazing—my friends think I'm crazy, but I'm so happy like this. I have learned that I can do relationships 'like the guys.' Men have been acting like this for ages. I think turnaround is fair play, don't you?"

3. **Panic.** "Hmmm, now that I've read the signs . . . Oh my, wait a minute. This is terrible! I never thought that I might have it, but actually, oh gosh, I think I might. But what does this say about me? What kind of person am I? Is there a cure? Does this mean I am going to be single for the rest of my life? Help!"

4. **Relief.** "That makes so much sense. For so long, I've thought that it might have been me all along. It's actually a huge relief to realize that other women are going through it, too. At least now I don't feel so alone."

Whether you're freaking out or are breathing a sigh of relief, glad to have finally pinned down the cause of your relationship troubles, you'll need to get more insight into the nature of your particular commitment issues. This is where some healthy self-assessment comes in. You can't possibly hope to get to the bottom of your anxiety until you accept all the fears and uncertainty driving your behavior. But remember, no matter how deep your commitment-phobia runs, it's hardly a life sentence. By no means does this condemn you to a life of solitude, unless, of course, you wouldn't have it any other way.

THE ULTIMATE COMMITMENT-PHOBE QUIZ

So are you or aren't you? While some women don't have even an inkling that they suffer from commitment anxiety, others of you are convinced that you're full-blown commitment-phobes. No use quizzing your friends, exes, or parents about it, either. While everyone will have some ideas about why you're single (grandmother: always slouching; sister: not enough color in wardrobe; best friend: way too picky), they're probably just as clueless as you are. So if you're ready to answer the big question once and for all, consider this quiz your saving grace.

1. **How often do you change your clothes in any given day?**
    A. Two to three times at least. I feel so gross wearing the same clothes all day.
    B. It depends. Some days more than others, especially if I have a date.
    C. Um . . . I guess I get dressed in the morning and that's pretty much it.

2. **Do you often describe yourself as having a "chameleon" personality?**
    A. Yeah, I say that all the time. I have a different personality every five minutes depending on where I am and whom I'm talking to.
    B. Sometimes, when I'm in a completely new place and I don't know anyone.
    C. What you see is what you get. I'm pretty much myself all the time.

3. **What is your parents' relationship like?**
    A. My whole family is totally nuts—and not in a good way.
    B. They've had many ups and downs, but they are still together.
    C. They're pretty happy all in all.

4. How many of your friends would you say are happily married?

    A. Ugh, next question. I don't have any married friends. How boring!

    B. A few seem pretty happy, but some are itching to get out.

    C. All my girlfriends are happy, ecstatic, and married. When's it going to be my turn?

5. How many jobs have you held in your life?

    A. I'm a compulsive job hopper. I can't seem to stay in one place for more than six months.

    B. The longest I've ever stayed at a job was one to two years.

    C. I've been working at the same place forever. I love it there!

6. Your best friend is getting married to a total schlub and you think she's making a huge mistake. You:

    A. Schedule an immediate intervention. Someone's got to help her before it's too late.

    B. Feel her out to see if she's happy and only say something if she expresses doubts.

    C. Don't say a word. Come on, can't you see how pretty she looks in her wedding dress?

7. How often do you switch hair colors and/or hairstyles?

    A. Every three to six months. I get bored with my look pretty quickly.

    B. About once a year. A little change now and then never hurts.

    C. I've pretty much had the same hair color and style since high school.

8. You've been seeing a guy for two weeks when he brings up the "exclusivity" talk. You:

    A. Feign a stomachache, double over in pain, and get out of there pronto!

    B. Tell the guy you need a little more time to get to know him.

    C. Pledge your complete loyalty and undying love to him.

9. What's your typical lunch during the workweek?

    A. Those awesome lunch buffets at my local deli. I load up my plate with a little bit of everything, from Chinese to Mexican food.

B. I have three favorite lunch spots that I usually alternate between.

C. I usually brown-bag my fave tuna salad or turkey sandwich.

10. **When your boyfriend of two months asks you to meet his friends, you:**

A. Ask him if any of them are hot.

B. Show up, but try to keep a little distance. You never know where this relationship is heading.

C. Get excited, buy a new outfit, and spend all your time trying to win his friends over.

11. **How long does it usually take for you to get bored in a relationship?**

A. A few weeks to a month.

B. Three to six months.

C. I rarely get bored in my relationships.

12. **Have you ever cheated on your partner?**

A. All the time, but it's not like we were exclusive or anything.

B. I'm ashamed to admit it, but yeah—once or twice.

C. Never. I'm a true-blue kind of girl.

13. **Which *Sex and the City* vixen are you most like?**

A. Samantha. My life is all about cocktails, business, and hookups.

B. Carrie. I'm always overanalyzing everything.

C. Charlotte. She's got family values and great taste in engagement rings.

14. **Your best friend calls and offers to buy tickets to your favorite rock band in a month. You:**

A. Decline. How can she expect me to know what I want to do in a month?

B. Agree to go. I can always sell the tickets if something better comes up.

C. Circle the date on your calendar. There's no way I'm missing this.

15. **Your friend just got a job at a bridal magazine. When she asks you to describe your perfect wedding, you:**
    A. Cringe inwardly, make a gagging sound, and ask her to change the subject.
    B. Admit you haven't thought about it much, but have a few ideas about size and location.
    C. Whip out the wedding collage that you've been assembling, complete with fabric swatches and favorite dresses.

16. **Your last single friend has just announced her engagement. You:**
    A. Sign up on Friendster or MySpace to find a new crew of single girlfriends. Who needs her, anyway?
    B. Feel a little sad, but wish her all the best.
    C. Bemoan my sorry lot and wish it were me who was getting married.

17. **When you're in a relationship, how often do your feelings change about your partner?**
    A. I honestly can't remember the last time I was in a relationship.
    B. A lot. One day I'm into him and the next day I'm not. What's up with that?
    C. I'm pretty consistent: if I like someone, there's not much he can do to turn me off.

18. **You've been working at a job for two years and your boss asks you to relocate to a new city. It means a huge promotion, but also leaving your boyfriend. What do you do?**
    A. Take the job, obviously.
    B. Ask my boyfriend if he would consider a long-distance relationship.
    C. I don't know. Probably stay where I am.

19. **When it comes to personal space, you need:**
    A. Tons of it. I could never live with a roommate or a guy.
    B. A little time alone to decompress.
    C. None. I would give up all the space in the world if it meant finding the right guy.

20. If someone said you were commitment-phobic, you would:
   A. Wonder what took them so long to realize it.
   B. Probably agree. I'm just so confused about everything.
   C. Laugh in their face. They don't know me at all.

21. What scares you most: ending up alone or not fulfilling your dream, whatever it may be?
   A. The dream.
   B. Um, do I have to choose one or the other?
   C. That's easy. What good is a stupid dream if I end up alone?

22. What kind of relationship films really do it for you?
   A. Something like *Mr. and Mrs. Smith* is more my speed.
   B. *When Harry Met Sally*—so much confusion, anxiety, and going back and forth.
   C. *Pretty Woman.* She gets the guy *and* the clothes. Need I say more?

Scoring: Assign 3 for every A, 2 for every B, and one for every C.

45–66 Points: Singularly Solo

There's no denying it: you're one certified commitment-phobe. And judging from your answers, you wouldn't have it any other way. There's no saying what led up to this current state of affairs. It could be that you're carrying around some baggage from your childhood, that you've had some painful relationships in the past, or that you just LOVE being single. In the end, only you can decide whether you're running away from something or just really enjoy being on your own. Of course, there is one sure way to find out, and that's to keep reading. Whether you become more commitment-phobic in the process or see some of yourself in any of the stories that follow, you'll definitely gain some much-needed perspective.

23–44 Points: Ambivalent Annie

What I'm about to say should come as no surprise: you definitely have your share of commitment issues. In fact, you're probably going back and forth as we speak—trying to figure out what to order for lunch, which hotel to book, or weighing up some poor guy's chances before kicking him out for being too . . . (you fill in the blank). When it comes to relationships, there's a part of you that thinks, "Damned if I do, damned if I don't." One minute you want more closeness, and the next you're breaking up a perfectly good relationship. But don't worry: the fact that you struggle with this issue is a good sign. At least you're motivated to figure out what's at the bottom of your uncertainty.

22 or Fewer Points: Commitment-Minded Connie

Can anyone say "commitment-obsessed"? You would rather die than end up alone, and you spend all your waking hours fantasizing about meeting the perfect guy. Not to begrudge you some frivolous fun planning a mock wedding or lighting your "love spell" candles, but consider that just because you *think* you want a commitment, that doesn't mean you're necessarily ready for one. In fact, all that compulsive thinking about commitment may actually be a way to sabotage real relationships from forming and developing naturally. We often avoid dealing with our personal issues about love and intimacy by escaping into a fantasy world where everything just happens magically. So while you may be enamored with the concept of a commitment, your gripping desire for it shows you may not be prepared to do the heavy lifting that relationships require.

YOUR CONSTANT COMPANION: COMMITMENT-PHOBIA THROUGH THE AGES AND STAGES

When it comes to commitment anxiety, no woman is safe. It can strike at any time, and when you least expect it—on a first date, when you first move in together, right before the wedding ceremony, and even when you're 50. The one thing you have to remember is that no one is immune. Most of us assume that once you get married or turn 35 that your commitment issues will just vanish into thin air. And while they may go into remission for a while, don't be surprised if you find them resurfacing again.

THE AGES

The 20-Something

With so many of us postponing marriage in our twenties, it's no surprise to find yourself riddled with commitment fears at this ripe young age. While your dear old ancestors may have been married with kids by the time they turned 24, no one would expect you to settle down so fast. There's your career, your education, and the prospect of playing the field to look forward to. With so many excuses for avoiding settling down in your twenties, it's surprising that anyone ever gets married before turning 30. Of course, it's easy to believe that as you get older your commitment issues will just magically disappear. And while that can happen, oftentimes our commitment-averse behavior only gets stronger with the passage of time.

THE CONFESSIONAL: Janet, 31

My commitment issues have definitely gotten worse with age and I don't really know why. I don't think it was such an issue when I was younger. When I was in my twenties, commitment didn't scare me because there was no permanence at that age. But now, I find that I'm less tolerant of people's idiosyncrasies and stuff. And I just can't imagine being with someone forever. It's definitely taken over my life, in a negative way. I don't really know why. I try not to overanalyze it because it stresses me out.

The 30-Something

During your fancy-free twenties, it might have seemed perfectly rational, even downright practical, to spurn the advances or proposals of all those eligible young men. But now as you get a little older (and by "older," I mean wiser), you've probably looked back on those years a little wistfully. If only you could have met that great ex-boyfriend ten years later. If only you knew then what you know now. While fantasizing about how things could have been different is a fun way to waste a rainy afternoon, these are, after all, fantasies we're talking about. No matter how great you think your college boyfriend was, it's important to realize that what worked for you in your twenties might not work in your thirties.

The other issue thirty-somethings face is that the older you get, the harder it becomes to merge with someone else. Being single can become a habit. Many of you will get used to living on your own, get set in your bachelorette ways, and find it tougher to compromise for the sake of a relationship.

What's more, just as you get comfortable being on your own, you'll also have to deal with the issue of the biological clock. Talk about a tailspin. It's not at all uncommon to find yourself struggling with the conflict between your need for independence and the desire to have children while you still can. But if you're convinced you want to have kids someday, your thirties are a great time to begin working through your fears of intimacy, permanence, and commitment. Or not, provided you're happy with where you are and where you're going.

THE DOCTOR IS IN

I think that women are raised to believe that we have timelines and we are supposed to get married or be in a relationship at a certain time or else something is wrong with us. We believe we have to have children by a certain age. We have these timelines imposed by social and cultural standards. Like that article that came out ten or fifteen years ago that if a woman's never been married by the age of 40 she's never going to get married. So there's this immense pressure. There's also an internal pressure that says that if I'm not interested in a relationship, people will think there's something wrong with me.

—*Debra Mandel, Ph.D.*

The 40-Something

By now, you've probably been through more than one relationship roller coaster. Whether you've been married before or have spent any amount of time single or in relationships, you most likely have a better understanding of your needs and expectations in a committed relationship. Most of you have gone through the struggle and have come out stronger and more certain of your choices in the process. Of course, right when you're most comfortable with your position in life, many of you will confront the fact that your biological clock is winding down. As a result, some of you may become more serious about the prospect of finding a committed relationship.

50s and Up

Many women in their fifties are either cruising for a new commitment after a divorce or separation or washing their hands of relationships entirely. Whether you've had positive experiences, negative ones, or a mixed bag, it's important to look at your situation from your new, more mature vantage point. After all, while you may have sworn off marriage earlier, who knows how your views have changed? The same goes for those of you who went from one relationship to another. It may be time to analyze whether your relationships reflect a desire for commitment or just a fear of being alone. The most important thing is not to come into this new, exciting stage in your life with the same expectations and habits. Many of you will find that dating a younger man may suddenly seem appealing, some will set off for new adventures as a single woman, and still others may find themselves relating to their partners on a deeper and more meaningful level. It's really anyone's guess.

THE STAGES

The Cohabiters

Living together can bring up a bevy of issues you never even thought existed. On one hand, it seems like a no-risk proposition: you can live with someone, get to know each other's quirks and habits, and figure out whether there's a future before signing on the dotted line. But for many women with commitment issues, moving in can feel like an enormous step in its own right. After all, there's putting down a deposit, signing a lease, and merging your valuables. It's all too easy to panic and want to bow out of the situation.

Even if you do finally make the leap into cohabitation, other issues will invariably creep in. While some of you will prefer to stay in living-together limbo, others will grow restless in this state of quasi-commitment. After all, while you're practically family and practically married, somehow you haven't made the decision to strike the lifetime bargain of "till death do us part." So without a more formal commitment in place, women with commitment issues are often tempted to bail out of the situation when things get rough rather than work out the inevitable kinks in the relationship.

THE CONFESSIONAL: Ann, 24

I didn't have commitment issues when we first moved in together. It was so exciting to finally be living on my own and having privacy with him. But then he got comfortable. No more romance, no more fun surprises, no more special moments. It got me wondering if he was the right guy for me, or if every guy does this once they get very used to you. So the commitment-phobia returned with a vengeance. Once you move in with a guy, they get comfortable and the spontaneity is gone. You know every word that is going to come out of his mouth before he even says it. You know every move he is going to make. That's when I get bored! It's also kind of like living with your parents in the sense that when I want to have a girls' night out, I have to let him know where I'm going, and if I come home too late I have to deal with his attitude.

The Pre-Engaged

If you think an engagement is stressful, you'd be surprised to find out that many women go through a crisis even before the question is ever popped. There's that point in every union when both people know that the relationship is either going down the toilet or down the aisle. Suddenly, every minor irritation that you would have overlooked before becomes a point of criticism and debate. You start questioning every little thing he does, from the way he chews his food to the sounds he makes in his sleep. If that wasn't enough to drive you crazy, you now have to give up control and let him do the proposing. No matter how liberated, many of you still want that magical proposal complete with bended knee, diamond ring, and a sunset setting. So for many women, the difficulty of reconciling their feminist ideals with their desire for a traditional engagement is sometimes enough to make them freak out, start questioning the relationship, and end up sabotaging a perfectly good union before it's even had time to hatch.

THE CONFESSIONAL: Janine, 30

My BF and I had been dating for two years and living together for one year when I suddenly realized I may be ready to get engaged. I've struggled with commitment issues all my life (my mother married twice and Dad is on his third marriage), so I was surprised to find myself thinking about making our relationship more permanent. He had brought up marriage and getting engaged throughout our time together, but I was never ready before. But once I was, I had no idea what to do. I thought about bringing up the topic, but I didn't know if I should do that or wait for him, which seemed kind of old-fashioned. It was the toughest seven months of my life, where I questioned everything from whether he loved me to whether I loved him. Finally, I decided enough was enough and just brought up the subject. In the end, as unromantic as it was, I'm glad I was the one to bring up marriage, since it forced me to confront my issues and consciously choose to be with him rather than just be swept along by the glamour of a gorgeous ring and a romantic proposal.

The Engaged

Once you've called everyone to break the big news and showed off your perfect princess-cut bauble, a girl has no choice but to come to down to earth—often with a loud thump. While many people assume that the engagement is supposed to be the happiest time of a woman's life, it's not at all uncommon to experience a whole slew of commitment issues during that period. Sure, there's the wedding planning, well-wishers, expensive gifts, and dreams of living happily ever after with your one and only. But for many of you, this is the ultimate breeding ground for commitment anxiety. Even if you've never experienced a fear of commitment and have been planning your wedding since birth, leave it to an engagement to bring out the hidden CP in even the giddiest wanna-be brides. For some of you, the proposal took up so much of your focus that you never really took the time to think about what married life would be like with your partner. That's why it often takes a proposal to make a woman finally sit back and analyze the situation without blinders. And while many relationships survive the heightened scrutiny, others fizzle under the glare.

THE DOCTOR IS IN

Many brides who have cold feet assume that because they're having negative feelings they should call off the wedding. There's a misconception that you're supposed to be on cloud nine once you get engaged. Every bride says she starts fighting with her fiancé more during the engagement process. You may have sat across from him a million times at dinner, but after you're engaged and he wears his baseball hat or puts his elbows on the table, you think, "Oh my God, will I be able to deal with that for the rest of my life?" Usually, it's not the guy or relationship that's the problem, but the anxiety of taking this next big step in your life.

—*Allison Moir-Smith, M.A.*

The Married

Think just because you're married, living in the suburbs, and have a few kids that you can avoid commitment-phobia? The good news is that some of you found that taking that leap into matrimony actually dispelled many of your commitment fears. After all, the world didn't end, the ground didn't open up, and lightning didn't strike when you uttered the words *I do*.

The bad news? Some of you have probably realized that your commitment issues have only become exacerbated with time. There's the newlywed considering annulment, the seven-year-itch scratcher who decides to take up with the pool guy, and even those who have been married for decades only to realize that they want out. Whether you went into the marriage with your eyes wide open or shut tight, once the deed was done, the reality and permanence of the situation probably came as quite a shock. No matter what your situation is, it's important to remember that sometimes commitment issues don't just disappear once you tie the knot.

THE CONFESSIONAL: Harold, 64

My ex-wife's first marriage lasted a couple of months and she bolted. Second marriage lasted a rocky ten years and she bolted. Her relationship with me lasted in total twenty-three years. However, on average she "left" the marriage every four years. I guess I was the one that kept pulling her back to the relationship. She's the mother of my children and I'm a family man. It sounds corny, but I believe in death do us part. She leaves me a note each and every time. There's no fight and no cold shoulders. Nothing that would give me a clue that she was about to snap again. Nothing that the children are able to pick up on that tells us that she is about to bail on us. Basically, all the notes say the same thing: "I love you, but I'm not in love with you."

THE DOCTOR IS IN

Women who are married or in long-term relationships can definitely be commitment-phobic on an intimacy level. You can be in a relationship technically—have a boyfriend or a husband—but are you really communicating on that soul level? Are you communicating on that deep, deep vulnerability, sharing that most inner part of your self, your frailties, your wounds, your essence of who you are, your most sacred part of who you are? Do you share that in a relationship or do you not? A lot of marriages don't have that, what I call a "soul marriage." People are still being self-protective, still being careful. They are still making sure their

The Divorced

"Once burned, twice shy" is probably your motto. It should come as no surprise that those of you who are separated or divorced have your fair share of issues about making another commitment. After all, if it didn't work out the first time, who's to say it will fare any better the second time around?

To add insult to injury, the divorced set also has to deal with exaggerated stats, with many studies suggesting that second or third marriages are more likely to fail than your first. But according to the 2002 National Survey of Family Growth, 54 percent of divorced women remarry in five years and only 25 percent of those marriages end within the first five years.

What's more, the stigma of divorce has significantly waned with the introduction of the "starter marriage" concept. Today it's almost expected to have your first marriage end, which lessens the isolation and sense of failure that many divorcees used to feel. So while it's true that many women get turned off to the institution for life, divorce is hardly the life sentence it used to be.

THE FIVE PANIC BUTTONS

No matter how cool, calm, and collected you normally are, there will come a time in every woman's life when commitment panic will set in. Whether you're on the verge of taking your first vacation together, getting your first apartment, or tying the knot, one or all of these panic buttons is likely to get pushed (and sometimes all at the same time). So instead of reaching for that paper bag until the hyperventilating and anxiety pass, read on to find out how to deactivate some of your most vulnerable trigger points.

THE CONFESSIONAL: Marie, 28

I feel like now that I'm married he's in the way of my life. Well, I would be going places, as far as traveling. I had plans to go with my friends. We were all going to take a trip to Spain and hang out because we don't have kids and we don't have any responsibilities that tie us down. I had everything planned out. I was going to finish paying off the car I love so much. And then I was going to live in Spain or Costa Rica, and travel with my friends who are musicians. But now that I'm married, the whole thing is canceled.

BUTTON #1: FEAR OF LOSING FREEDOM

Whenever I ask someone why they love living in New York, the conversation invariably goes something like this:

> *New Yorker:* "That's easy. It's the only place I can get coffee or a bagel or a slice of pizza at five o'clock in the morning."
> *Me:* "So how often do you do that?"
> *New Yorker:* "Oh, never, but I like to know that the option is there."

When it comes to our attitudes about personal freedom in relationships, the same logic often applies. Committing to someone means that the option of flying off at a moment's notice to Paris with some gorgeous guy we just met no longer exists. And while that probably would never have happened in the first place, when you're single, the possibility is there.

While single life does offer some liberties that relationships do not, commitment can also provide certain freedoms, such as freedom from emotional insecurity, freedom from worrying about your love life, and freedom to pursue activities as part of a couple. The fact is that many women report having more freedom to pursue their interests and goals now that their single years have come to an end. Just imagine how much free time you would have if you combined all those hours spent browsing online dating profiles, selecting the right outfit, and fretting over your love life.

BUTTON #2: FEAR OF DIVORCE

Ask any commitment-phobe and she'll cite divorce as her number one fear, for good reason: the numbers seem to be climbing and the media are constantly harping on the fact that, at best, our unions have only a fifty-fifty chance of survival. But as with most stats, this one, too, is grossly exaggerated. According to Joshua R. Goldstein, associate professor of sociology and public affairs at Princeton University's Office of Population Research, insufficient government studies during times of high divorce rates have led people to believe that there is a higher chance of divorce than really exists. Data from the 2002 National Survey of Family Growth peg the failure rate at only 33 percent (first marriages ending in separation or divorce after ten years).

In the end, our perceptions of a high divorce rate are actually a self-fulfilling prophecy. As new numbers are released showing that the rate is dropping, don't be surprised to find your optimism about commitment returning. Besides, it's counterproductive to fear the D-word. Excuse me for this moment of morbidness, but just because we know that we'll all die someday doesn't mean that we will decide to stop living. The same goes for the other D-word. Just because there's a chance that you'll divorce, that doesn't mean you can't give commitment a shot.

BUTTON #3: FEAR OF BECOMING AN ADULT

Look, no one said growing up was fun, easy, or especially exciting. With more than 18 million people ages 18–34 still living at home with their parents, this generation is by no means in any hurry to grow up. Admit it—most of our ideas of what it means to be an "adult" revolve around seeing our parents struggle to pay their mortgage and act as 24/7 chauffeurs, carting us around from one after-school activity to another. Not exactly an enticing scenario for a generation of women weaned on cocktails, Sunday brunches, and sample sales. But what's the alternative? That we'll end up doing the same thing day in and day out until we turn 70. While having a spring in your step may be easy when you're single, fancy-free, and full of possibilities, commitment doesn't mean the end of all that.

THE DOCTOR IS IN

Becoming a part of a committed relationship is stepping into adulthood. I work with brides who are age 20 and are dealing with this and brides who are 50 years old who are also dealing with this. It has nothing to do with chronological age. One client I had was 49 years old. For her, getting married was the ultimate step into adulthood, and she was scared. Your girlhood, your single life, your solely independent nature are on the line. To be in a relationship is to become interdependent, and that's frightening for many of us.

—*Allison Moir-Smith, M.A.*

BUTTON #4: FEAR OF REJECTION

Oftentimes our fear of commitment has to do with an immense fear of being abandoned, rejected, and cast aside. Many of you have probably gone through painful experiences in which you opened up to someone only to be rejected. It's easy to react to this pain by shutting down emotionally, preemptively breaking off relationships, or avoiding dating all together.

Columbia University psychologist Geraldine Downey, Ph.D., found that some individuals are more prone to feeling rejected than others, even if the other person did nothing to make them feel that way. So if you suffer from rejection sensitivity, it's important that you deal with past issues and really understand how they inform your current behavior. The bottom line is this: if you're constantly on the lookout for signs of rejection, you may end up creating the very reality you fear most.

THE DOCTOR IS IN

There are two major fears. One fear is that she is going to be controlled by a man and the other is that he'll abandon her. At the bottom of all our fears is an attempt to protect the self—ego—from being hurt. And so what we do is say, "I never want to get hurt like that again; therefore I will avoid a situation that looks anything like the one I got hurt in." Again, it's looking at the past and saying this is what happened and this is what's likely to happen in the future.

—*Dr. Deborah Anapol*

BUTTON #5: FEAR OF LOSING CAREER/IDENTITY

You've worked hard all your life, and there's no denying that what you do for a living informs your sense of identity and self-worth. Long hours at the office, business travel, and years spent getting advanced degrees have made it doubly difficult for many of you to focus on relationships. As a result, you've become accustomed to compromising for the benefit of your professional life, not your personal life. Many of you ask yourselves tough questions every day:

- "Will I have to give up my job?"
- "Will I have to discontinue my education?"
- "Could I still travel on business at a moment's notice?"
- "Would having children impede my professional progress?"

It's not surprising that many of you worry about the impact a committed relationship or marriage will have on your career. After all, many of our mothers had to give up their jobs and financial independence once they got married and had kids. But today's economic and social picture is much different.

Kiss and Run

55

According to researchers Waite and Nielsen, in the 1960s only one third of households were dual-income. Today, the number is much higher, with over two thirds of all households falling into this category. Not only do most men today expect you to continue working after the vows are exchanged, they'll be pretty miffed if you don't. After all, housing prices are still rising, credit card debt is at an all-time high, and education costs are skyrocketing. So unless you're marrying Donald Trump, there's much less chance that you will lose your career or identity once you get married. It's simply not a luxury many of you will be able to afford.

THE DOCTOR IS IN

Sometimes people will use their careers as a way of avoiding facing that they have commitment fears, and that's very typical with men. And increasingly, as women climb the ladder in the workplace and there's more permission for women to make career a number one priority, you see that symptom in women more frequently as well.

—*Debra Mandel, Ph.D.*

EXERCISE: THE PAST-LOVES POSTMORTEM

If you have any hope of getting over your commitment anxiety, you're going to have to 'fess up to your past and take some responsibility. It might hurt to say "I was wrong," but it's better than feeling like a victim and constantly saying "I was wronged." After all, there's a certain dignity to admitting your ambivalence and being accountable for your romantic choices. No matter how you recollect your past, you'd be surprised how many of your relationships were marred by your own commitment issues. Complete this exercise to find out exactly what role you played in past relationships.

Your three greatest loves/significant relationships were:

1. _____

_____

2. _____
   _____

3. _____
   _____

In each relationship, what factors contributed to the breakup?

1. _____
   _____

2. _____
   _____

3. _____
   _____

What could you have done differently in each relationship?

1. _____
   _____

2. _____
   _____

3. _____
   _____

What are the top three things you would want your exes to remember about you?

1. _____
   _____

2. _____
   _____

3. _____
   _____

In what ways did you give up on each relationship before it ended (cheating, withholding, arguing, etc.)?

1. _____
   _____

2. _____
   _____

3. _____
   _____

When did you first realize that the relationship had no future?

1. _____
   _____

2. _____
   _____

3. _____
   _____

If any of your past loves came back right now wanting to reconcile, you would probably:

1. _____
   _____

2. _____
   _____

3. _____
   _____

For each past love, write up a short description of what your life would have been like had you stayed together.

1. _____
   _____

2. _____

_____

3. _____

_____

Write a few words about how you think each relationship affected your current attitude toward love, commitment, and marriage.

1. _____

_____

2. _____

_____

3. _____

_____

 On a separate sheet of paper, use the information above to write a letter to every one of your past loves. I don't care if they cheated on you, broke your heart, or disappeared without as much as a phone call. This is not the time to vent or lay blame. This is about *you*. Focus on your role in the relationship. Describe to each ex where you are now in your life and what your goals are for the future. Try to identify some of the conflicts, fears, and vulnerabilities that plagued you at that time, and share these insights with your ex-partner. And don't forget to sign off by writing something positive about the relationship: what you've learned, what you discovered about yourself, and how you've grown since.

THE THREE BIGGIES: YES, I HEARD YOU!

While many of your backgrounds, situations, and attitudes about commitment are vastly different, it's amazing how much all you women have in common, including your top three questions. You'd be surprised how many of you voiced the following concerns.

1. "Is it commitment-phobia or just that I haven't met the right person?"

I hear this one all the time. Not only is it the most common question, it's also the most interesting. "Am I alone because I want it that way or because I haven't met the right guy?" Hmmm . . . kind of makes you think. Many of you are convinced that the reason you're single is that you just haven't met the right guy. You believe that your married or committed friends just drew a better number in the love lottery and that once you meet the right person all your commitment issues will simply vanish into thin air.

It's fair to say that some of you just can't wrap your mind around the fact that you have commitment issues. In fact, "I haven't met the right person" is the most common rationalization women use to avoid dealing with their anxiety. But meeting someone who's right for you is not just about luck and good timing, it's about being emotionally and psychologically ready to make a lasting connection. There may have been plenty of guys you've met who could have been contenders, but you were probably not in the right head space to recognize them. In the end, commitment issues won't just go away when you meet the man you've been dreaming of. In fact, meeting the right person may just make them even worse.

THE DOCTOR IS IN

When a woman is desperately seeking a partner and unable to find one over a period of time, that's a suggestion that there's fear there, maybe of commitment, maybe of other things. There's nothing wrong with saying, "I don't really want to be in a relationship right now." But if you're actively looking and not finding, you may be unconsciously saying no to a relationship. Again, rather than taking the responsibility and saying, "I don't want a partner," it's very convenient to find there's no man that's good enough for me.

—*Dr. Deborah Anapol*

Elina Furman

2. "Do I want to get married or do I just want to be asked?"

You remember your last dating debacle—when the guy showed up late, talked about his ex all night, and then tried to maul you at the door. Well, the only thing worse than going on a second date was when that guy you hated so much didn't call. It's a case of "I don't want to be with him, but why doesn't *he* want to be with *me*?" Many of us may not necessarily want to date someone, but that doesn't mean we don't still want them to desire us.

It's the same line of reasoning that leads many of you to think that you're ready for a commitment when all you're really ready for is a proposal. You may not even particularly like the guy, but you figure, *Well, the least he could do is ask.* Oh, just admit it. I don't care how much of a feminist you are, how much money you make, and how much you say you don't care about it. In every woman, there's a small part of her that wants to be "picked." It goes back to our younger years, when being invited to the prom or asked out by our crush bestowed a certain amount of social respect or legitimacy on our awkward teen selves. And while it's okay to want to feel desired, special, and vied after, try not to confuse your ego or a pretty ring with a desire to get married.

THE CONFESSIONAL: Kelly, 31

I was engaged to someone and I was freaking out. I mean, he—my ex-fiancé—kind of just sprang the question on me. It was his idea. It wasn't like I wanted to get married. He thought it was going to change him, and I thought it was the right thing to do. Mostly I was just like, "Oh my God, someone spent $8,000 on a ring for me!" I was like, "No one has ever given me something like that." I was beside myself. Every time I looked at it, I was like, "Oh my God." But ultimately, I had to call off the engagement.

3. "Do I want to be committed or do my parents, friends, and society want me to be?"

Consciously choosing to be single is one of the toughest decisions anyone can make. After all, we have a myriad of voices telling us we're not complete without a man and that we're still going to be judged by our relationship status no matter how well we do in life. That's why many of you will act as if you're looking for a commitment when all you really want to do is relax and take some time out for yourself.

It's very likely that many of you don't quite see the point of making a long-term commitment or getting married. But even if everything in your body is screaming out for independence and solitude, the constant barrage of messages from your friends, parents, and the media is bound to confuse you. That's why it's so important that you filter all these social directives so that you can begin to separate your own needs and desires from the millions of voices screaming, "If you want any sort of life at all, you'd better get married by 35." No matter what everyone else wants for you, you need to give yourself the freedom to pursue your own course, whether it is a popular choice or not. In the end, committing to being single, at least for now, is a decision that deserves to be honored and respected.

THE DOCTOR IS IN

I think that a recent phenomenon is that people have given themselves permission to be single. I think it's always been an option, but there's always been so much prejudice against people who stay single, so very few people have had the courage to admit it. It could be parents or other friends who are always telling them that they are wrong to stay single. There is this norm that says there's something not right if you haven't committed by a certain age. But if that's the lifestyle that works for you and you consider it a choice, then it doesn't have to be a disease.

—*Dr. Michael S. Broder*

SO NOW YOU KNOW!

I hope by now you have a better idea of whether you're a raging commitment-phobe or just your run-of-the-mill commitment-avoider. No doubt all this talk about being confused, ambivalent, and uncertain is making you feel a little up in the air. Many of you are probably anxious to fix your issues so you can go on to enjoy healthy, committed relationships. And rightly so! All the awareness in the world won't do you a bit of good unless you're ready to start taking action.

But before you jump into the next section stilettos first, take a moment and analyze how you feel about the fact that you may be commitment-phobic. Are you scared, anxious, relieved, or all of the above? No matter what you discover about yourself in the next chapters, remember you're perfectly normal. So now that you know you're a commitment-phobe (and please don't freak out), read on to find out exactly which category you fall into.

The Nitpicker

LAID-BACK, LOW-MAINTENANCE SF, 110 lbs., 31, seeking 34- to 35-year-old professional (doctors, bankers okay . . . no lawyers or accountants please). Must be at least 5' 11" and no more than 190 lbs. Must have graduated from a top-25 school (no Yalies) with minimum grade point average 3.8. Recreation: sailing, Frisbee in the park, movies (indies only), no Rollerbladers, antique shopping a must, some knowledge of 19th-century French literature preferred. Hobbies: racquetball, southern Italian cooking, coin collectors welcome, must have traveled extensively except no travel in Asia in past 4 years (bird flu). Past relationships: have slept with maximum 15 girls, 5 of which lasted longer than 3 months. Three serious exes max (must live in different cities). Sexual habits: not too dominant or passive. Must enjoy pleasing a woman. Prefer sex 3 times a week during first 6 months, and twice a week thereafter. No fetishists or perverts. In a nutshell, I'm looking for someone like me, laid-back and able to adapt to any situation (be just as comfortable at a black-tie gala as you are rummaging through the dumpster for my lost valuables). Please submit current photo (color 5 X 10 full-body shot), high school photo, father's photo, 3 letters of recommendation, tax returns from the past 5 years, and a 500-word essay on what makes you a unique and special person.

$\mathcal{E}$ ver since Goldilocks trespassed through the Bears' house, we girls have been accused of extreme selectivity to the point of nitpickiness. This one's too big! Too small! This one's too cold! Too hot! Whether it's you or your friends, you've probably made and heard your fair share of complaints about the opposite sex. Weird accent, no hair, too short, big ears, mangled cuticles . . . there are a million qualities that can send you running for the door.

Sometimes it seems as if the whole world is against you, too. When it comes to your pickiness—parents, friends, coworkers, siblings—everyone's got an opinion. "That Jane," they say, shaking their heads in resignation, "no one's ever good enough for her." And you just sit there, hands folded neatly in your lap, wondering, "Is it too much to ask that a grown man not wear his pants up to his elbows? Is it too much to ask that he not chew with his mouth open?" Besides, just what's wrong with being so picky anyway? What's wrong with wanting someone to be your soul mate—your equal in every way? What's wrong with wanting someone to pick up your dry cleaning, someone to walk your dog, someone to make you laugh on cue, someone to solve the Middle East crisis, someone to run out for Häagen-Dazs on command, someone to . . . ? Okay, you get the idea.

Whereas some women don't ask enough from a relationship, happy if the guy is clean-shaven, polite, and has no criminal record, Nitpickers often go way overboard in the high expectations department. But that's the whole problem: they are so afraid to commit or even begin a real relationship that they compile a list of impossible requirements that no one will ever be able to meet. After all, the more complicated the order, the more difficult it is to fill it. And if by some chance a man does manage to break through the three-date hurdle to make it to the one-month mark, well, then the Nitpicker comes up with a slew of new, even more stringent requirements, challenges, and expectations.

THE CONFESSIONAL: Paige, 26

Being picky never used to bother me at all. In fact, I kind of prided myself on it. I would go out with a guy, date for a few weeks, and then find

something terribly wrong with him. Finally, I met one guy and I thought I was really falling in love. Then he brought up moving in together and out of nowhere I got this weird feeling. I couldn't stand to be around him. Everything began bothering me—the smell of his apartment, his messy closet, his toenail clippings everywhere. I just really couldn't see this thing going anywhere. So I broke up with him, even though I think a part of me is maybe still in love with him.

Faced with the prospect of falling in love, Nitpickers immediately begin to overanalyze the situation, frantically evaluating every little thing he did or said until you hit upon that perfect deal breaker, excuse, turn-off, or pet peeve that will finally end the relationship once and for all. "Phew," you breathe, "that was close." A perfectly normal guy has just become another name on your now mile-long list of could-have-beens, should-have-beens, but will-never-bes.

The question is, are you really ready to cast off your nitpicky ways for good? Are you ready to face up to the fact that your behavior could be just another way of avoiding commitment? Even if you answered yes to those questions, be aware that there's no overnight cure. You have a lifetime of criticizing, picking apart, and deconstructing behind you, and it's going to take time to change your ways. Fortunately, your case is not a terminal one. If you're serious about change, rest assured, there is a cure.

 QUIZ: PICKY OR *TOO* PICKY?

When it comes to pickiness, there are absolutely no absolutes. Some of you may have set the bar way too high, while others may still be receptive enough to recognize a good guy when you see one. So how do you rate on the picky scale? Take this quiz to find out.

1. **Your coworker sets you up on a blind date. When you arrive for drinks at the local hot spot, he's wearing a seersucker suit and matching pastel socks in the middle of winter. You:**

A. Bolt for the door before he sees you.

B. Figure, "What's one drink?" and prepare to be bored out of your mind.

C. Smile and introduce yourself—this guy has to have confidence to pull off that look.

2. **How would you best describe what you're looking for in a guy?**

   A. The three R's: rich, ravishing, and ready.

   B. As good as it gets: good-looking, good in bed, good to me.

   C. Attractive to me, fun to be around, and honest.

3. **How do you want your friends to react when they first meet your boyfriend?**

   A. Green with envy. Is that bad?

   B. Just a tiny bit jealous, but mostly happy that I found a good match.

   C. I don't care. I'm just happy to be with someone I like.

4. **You've been seeing a guy for two months. Everything is going great, until he does this one particular thing. What's your ultimate deal breaker?**

   A. Asks me to pay.

   B. Forgets to call me on one or two occasions.

   C. Is dishonest or mean to someone.

5. **How many first dates have you been on in the past three months?**

   A. More than fifteen. It takes a special man to get to the second-date mark.

   B. More than five. I have to be very attracted to him to accept a second date.

   C. Less than five. I usually go on two dates with someone before I rule him out.

6. **You're dining at your favorite restaurant. How long does it usually take you to order a meal?**

   A. Until the waiter's eyes glaze over—"on the side, hold this, substitute that." *What?* I like what I like!

   B. Just a minute—or two. I only have a few dietary specifications.

   C. I'm pretty fast.

7. What's your idea of the perfect first date?

A. Being picked up in a nice car, drinks at a chic hotel, dinner with a view, followed by VIP club entry for late-night dancing.

B. Drinks and dinner at a nice restaurant work for me.

C. Hanging out with friends or going to a party, and then somewhere quiet to talk.

8. If you were to draft a list of must-have qualities for your future mate, how long would it be?

A. At least three pages.

B. One page tops.

C. Maybe five to ten lines.

9. We all know that size matters. What kind of size matters most to *you*?

A. The size of his wallet.

B. The size of his . . . feet.

C. The size of his heart.

10. How many men have you dated who actually measured up to your standards?

A. Big zero. I haven't met a man yet who could meet all my expectations.

B. A couple. With a little work, they may have even been perfect.

C. Plenty. There are many great men out there, I just haven't found the one for me.

Scoring: To calculate your final score, assign a point value to each answer: 3 for every A, 2 for every B, and 1 for every C. Now add it all up to see how you rank.

23–30 Points: Get a Grip, Sister!

I don't mean to be picky, but really, do you have to be so picky? Have you ever thought of heading down to the Mattel toy factory and asking them to customize your own special blow-up doll, because that may be the only way you can get what you're looking for? While setting goals and having standards are important, you don't want to get carried away by unrealistic expectations. After all, would *you* be able to match all the criteria you set for your dates? If you're not careful, your attitude can lead to major disappointment in the love department. Why not take a good long look at yourself for a change? Do you really want a relationship? Is there something lacking in your own life that you need a guy to bring? No one's saying you shouldn't set your sights high, but a reality check every now and then could do you a world of good.

15–22 Points: Rein It In

When it comes to the opposite sex, no one would accuse you of not knowing what you want. You're picky, but not to a fault. That's the good news. The bad news is that you sometimes go for style over substance. No one can blame you for holding out for a hottie, but you may just end up overlooking great sexy guys who need a few dates to come out of their shell. All in all, you're doing great—getting out there, having fun, and mixing it up. But when you're ready to stop playing the field, take some time to reevaluate what you want versus need from your partner. You'd be surprised at how these things change over time.

14 or Fewer Points: Keep It Up

With your open and laid-back attitude, it's a wonder you're still single. When it comes to love, no one has to tell you that substance always wins out in the end and that the best relationships take time to develop. You're open enough to give a variety of guys a chance, and you understand that if it doesn't work out, at least you have given it your best shot. You're just the kind of girl most guys are looking for: low-key, confident, and serious about the things that matter. What's left to say? We should all be so lucky as you!

NITPICKER PROTESTS: "I'M NOT PICKY, I JUST . . ."

I know, I know . . . You're not nitpicky, you're just selective. You're not nitpicky, you just like what you like. Believe me, I've heard it all before. If you're convinced that you're the exception to every Nitpicker rule, you may be in for a surprise. Read on to find the answers to some of the most common Nitpicker protests. Repeat after me: "I'm not picky, I just . . ."

1. **"I Just Have Standards."** Quality control is all well and good. If it wasn't for those little inspectors sticking their noses into the assembly line, you could never be sure you were getting what you paid for. So when it comes to quality control for your own love life, aren't you entitled to exact the same stringent inspec-

tion reserved for your toothpaste? After all, with so many guys out there, you can afford to throw a few irregular models back into the bin every now and then. But before you do, consider those gorgeous discount shoes you found in the bargain bin. You figured, "What's a little nick here and there?" and were smart enough to grab those babies before someone else did. After all, you're not one to let a minor manufacturing error stand in the way of you and your designer footwear. Well, the same law applies to men. While he may have some minor flaws and scuffs, while he may not meet your every standard for quality assurance, he may have other things going for him—such as fit, flair, and function. So instead of freaking out because his teeth are not Invisalign perfect, why not try to focus on how good it feels to unearth a designer treasure in the bargain bin?

THE CONFESSIONAL: Leslie, 28

Everyone tells me I'm too picky: my guy friends, my girlfriends, my parents. But I've always been this way. It takes me forever to decide what to wear, what to eat, what to get my friends for their birthdays. And when it comes to dating, I'm impossible. I always look at every date and think I deserve a lot better. Recently, I'm thinking my pickiness is becoming even worse. I met this great guy. He was funny, intelligent, came from a good family—everything I was looking for. The problem is, he wasn't that well-read. I pride myself on being somewhat literary and didn't think I could spend the rest of my life with someone who's only read one book in the last year.

2. **"I Just Haven't Met the Right Guy."** Well, that's like saying, "I'm not depressed, I just haven't found anything to be happy about." Like happiness, finding the right guy is all a matter of perspective. There have probably been a million guys who have fit some if not most of your criteria—guys you may have ignored while you were too busy pining away for the broad-shouldered Lothario staring at himself in the mirror. So how do you know if it's the guys you're meeting (better yet, *not* meet-

ing) or the fact that you're too picky? Since you can't go back in time and recount every detail of your romantic castoffs, you'll just have to take a leap of faith. That's right, you'll have to make a commitment to stop being picky and see what happens. And if you suddenly find yourself meeting all these great guys and singing "It's Raining Men," don't be too surprised. They were there all along.

THE DOCTOR IS IN

A lot of people would rather blame their predicament on circumstances rather than the fact that they've set it up for themselves to not meet the kind of person they want to meet. It's very possible that you can have whatever degree of standards you want to have and it's very possible that you will not meet anyone in this lifetime who will match them. But that's a choice you have to make. You have to realize that if you want somebody who does not exist, you are not going to meet anyone.

—*Dr. Michael S. Broder*

3. **"I Just Get Turned Off Easily."** When it comes to chemistry, there's no bargaining with your libido, is there? Either you are or you aren't attracted to someone. It's not like you can talk yourself into arousal or anything, right? Well, don't be so sure. After all, there are millions of women out there who weren't attracted to their guys at first, only to find that they now can't keep their hands off them. While attraction is important (okay, we're talking non-negotiable), the things you are turned on by today may not be the same things you're attracted to tomorrow. Think about it. As a kid, I used to hate sushi, mustard, and pickles. Everyone kept telling me, "You can't know if you like it until you try it." And as much as I protested at the time, they were right. Now I'm addicted to all three (not in the same sitting, of course). As you mature, so do your tastes and preferences. And while you may not want to taste-test every man who comes your way, you may want to occasionally reevaluate what's appealing to you.

TESTY, TESTY!

Think your dates have to jump through hoops and over hurdles to pass your love test? You're not alone. Plenty of Nitpickers like yourself have devised complicated questionnaires that even card-carrying MENSA members would have a hard time passing. Don't deny it! No matter what he says, you'll probably still find something wrong with him.

You: "So what's your relationship with your mother like?"
Him: "I love my mother. She's one of the greatest women I know."
Nitpicker verdict: Mama's boy.

You: "So are you career-driven?"
Him: "Yes, I'm passionate about my work as a lifestyle counselor. I teach people how to balance their work and personal lives."
Nitpicker verdict: Obsessive workaholic.

You: "So when was your last relationship?"
Him: "I was dating a wonderful woman for three years, but we grew apart."
Nitpicker verdict: Still in love with his ex.

You: "So what do you do for fun?"
Him: "Um, let's see. I love doing crosswords, hanging out at the coffee shop with friends, going to movies—that kind of thing."
Nitpicker verdict: Slacker couch potato.

TOP NITPICKER HANG-UPS

If you're feeling a little bit picked on by this chapter, that's okay. It's high time you scrutinized yourself as carefully as you do the men in your life. And don't worry, you're in good company. There are many women like you with varying degrees of nitpickiness. If you're in doubt, see if you've ever been hung up by any of these common hang-ups.

1. The Shopping List from Hell

After years on the singles circuit, you've probably dated enough men to realize what it is you do and do not want. Problem is, with every year and so many dates, your list has probably grown longer and longer. And while it's important to have a general idea of what you're looking for, sticking too closely to your shopping list can prevent you from meeting the very men you're looking for. Let's say you're looking for a partner with a graduate degree. What you're really seeking is someone brainy and ambitious. In eliminating all men without college degrees, you may discount the self-made entrepreneur who dropped out of college (think Bill Gates) or the creative visionary who skipped college to become a successful writer. I know that there are many facets of dating life that mirror the shopping experience, but let's not carry the analogy too far, ladies. No matter how specific your list of criteria is, you simply can't order up a male specimen like you would dinner take-out.

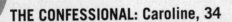

THE CONFESSIONAL: Caroline, 34

Ever since I was old enough to write, I've been compiling a list of all the qualities I want in a husband. The list is pretty long—it has about 150 items by now—but it's a great way for me to keep in mind what I'm looking for. So far I've only met two guys who had maybe a third of all the items on the list, but in the end it just didn't work out. Still, I'm very optimistic. I hope that one day I'll find the guy who has everything on my list, my one true soul mate.

2. The Blemish Bylaw

We all get unsightly blemishes from time to time. And once you spot it in the mirror, it's almost impossible to focus on anything but that. You stare, you pick, you moan to yourself—there's just no getting away from it. The Blemish Bylaw is simple to remember: *look and you shall find.* If you look hard enough and long enough at something, it's bound to become larger than life. The same law applies to the men in your life. Whether his nose is too pointy or his ears too large, you probably tried to ignore it at first. But now you find yourself transfixed by it, staring at the unsightly characteristic as if you were in a state of deep hypnosis.

We're all guilty of focusing on the little things at the expense of the big picture. Having had many similar reactions to minor imperfections myself, I can certainly relate to the Nitpicker dilemma. But by focusing on minor, insignificant details, you can end up leaving perfectly compatible men by the wayside. It's the old missing-the-forest-for-the-trees phenomenon. Think about it. If you're too busy staring at his bitten-down cuticles, you may miss the fact that he volunteers at the hospital every week (and has a nice butt). On the flip side, if you're all wrapped up in bonding over your mutual love of opera, you may fail to notice that he didn't thank the waitress once during the entire dinner. It's a costly mistake that can lead you to dismiss good guys and accept those who are lacking fundamentally important traits.

3. The Mr. Darcy Complex

Stop me if you've heard this one: a slightly frumpy, disheveled, but cute single gal meets the perfect male specimen—any variation on Brad Pitt, Johnny Depp, or Colin Firth will do—and after a series of near misses and romantic escapades, the two realize they're meant to be and live happily ever after.

While I'm usually one of the first suckers in line for any romantic comedy or epic love story, Nitpickers have a tendency to take these films' lessons a little too literally. I mean, what mortal man can honestly compete with these finely chiseled heroes?

A study conducted by Rutgers University's National Marriage Project found that 88 percent of single men and women ages 20 to 29 believe that there is one person out there destined to be their soul mate. And an outrageously large 94 percent agreed with this statement: "When you marry, you want your spouse to be your soul mate, first and foremost."

With Hollywood's promise of instant soul mate recognition and the idea that you're destined to meet the one perfect man who'll fulfill *all* your needs, you're bound to be disappointed

Elina Furman

when you meet those run-of-the-mill guys who are great but bear no resemblance to their silver-screen counterparts. Here are some of the most popular myths you may need to debunk:

Hollywood Myth #1: Mr. Perfect is out there waiting for you, if only you can find him.

Hollywood Myth #2: Once you find Mr. Perfect, you'll just instantly know it was meant to be.

Hollywood Myth #3: Mr. Perfect isn't perfect, but his faults are so cute you'll just magically overlook them.

Hollywood Myth #4: The nice, reliable guy you're with right now is never the one you're supposed to end up with. Leave it to Mr. Perfect to come along and show you the error of your ways.

THE DOCTOR IS IN

People walk into relationships all the time thinking they are going to be with Prince Charming. You know, the prince with no flaws. That's a sure-fire way to have disappointment in a relationship. I think the concept of a soul mate is lovely. But I never knew exactly what that meant. It's a great fairy-tale kind of phenomenon, but a soul mate implies the idea that somebody is going to be able to read your mind and know your spirit inside and out without you having to communicate. And that's a recipe for disaster in a relationship. Get realistic about what you can expect from a partner and what you can actually contribute in a relationship.

—*Debra Mandel, Ph.D.*

While the film industry does crank out some entertaining fare, let's get one thing straight: no one is perfect, not even you! Okay, you may be a celebrated concert pianist, an Olympic gold medalist, or on your way to winning the Mother Teresa award, but even with all these accolades under your belt, I'm sure you have a few minor faults. It's easy to go on believing you're perfect when you're used to living on your own. After all, you probably don't fight with yourself over the remote control, don't nag yourself to do the dishes, and never give yourself the silent treatment. Everyone is perfect when they are alone. It's when we decide to commit to someone that we realize, "Uh-oh, I guess I'm not so perfect after all."

THE PERFECT BOYFRIEND MIXER GAME

How many times have you said, "If only I could combine Tom, Eric, and Kevin into one guy"? Well, now you can! You have to admit that it's a little bit ridiculous to expect one man to have all the qualities you're looking for, but indulge me for the sake of this exercise. Just picture your past three boyfriends and enter a description for each category—for example, wavy hair, average physique, wry sense of humor. Now pick out four qualities from each boyfriend to complete the perfect guy column. While the perfect guy will probably never materialize, at least now you can create one on paper.

Boyfriend 1	Boyfriend 2	Boyfriend 3	Perfect Boyfriend

Name	Name	Name	Name
Hair:	Hair:	Hair:	
Face:	Face:	Face:	
Body:	Body:	Body:	
Height:	Height:	Height:	
Humor:	Humor:	Humor:	
Sensitivity:	Sensitivity:	Sensitivity:	

Brains:	Brains:	Brains:	
Ambition:	Ambition:	Ambition:	
Sex:	Sex:	Sex:	
Communication:	Communication:	Communication:	
Character:	Character:	Character:	
Values:	Values:	Values:	

4. Jet-setting Homebodies, Attentive Workaholics, and Other Dating Paradoxes

One of the biggest hang-ups Nitpickers face is enforcing demands that are inherently contradictory. Let's face it—there are very few ambitious, successful men who'll insist on spending all their time with us. They're too busy chasing their millions. And you'd be hard pressed to find a spontaneous, jet-setting party boy who likes to spend most of his nights cuddled up on a couch with you. Or what about a masculine guy's guy who also happens to love chick flicks and poetry slams? Some traits are just mutually exclusive. It's either one or the other.

This gets us back to the idea of the perfect person. We want someone gentle but assertive, outgoing but introspective, laugh-out-loud funny but with a serious side. A girl can dream, can't she? The problem with this train of thought is that it puts an inordinate amount of pressure on the men you date.

Of course, you may be asking, "But why can't I find someone who's as multifaceted as I am?" Well, no one says you can't. But once you become more aware of the contradictions in your romantic requirements, you'll finally stop chasing wealthy, successful types when all you're looking for is a kind and gentle guy who'll read you to sleep every night.

THE CONFESSIONAL: Lauren, 29

I have a huge network of friends—pretty much all of my girlfriends from college as well as a lot of new ones I've met while living in the city. I've always dated these very athletic, all-American types, and when we're out at a bar, my friends always know who my type is right away. When I met David, I really never thought it would go anywhere. He was shorter than I'm used to and a little bit out of shape. But we had really good chemistry, and I decided I could look past these flaws. Problem was, I was still a little bit embarrassed to introduce him to my friends. I just know how judgmental they could be, and I was worried that they would think I settled. I think David sensed something was up, because he ended up breaking up with me a few weeks later. I think I may have really hurt his feelings.

5. Survey Says: The Post-Date Gabfest

As every Nitpicker knows, half the fun of dating is the recap with our friends. Some Nitpickers love to go over every detail, laughing at the poor, unsuspecting guys over lunches and dinners with their much cooler, much more with-it gal pals. Okay, so we all care what our friends think. Go ahead, sue us! But it's not like you're the only one.

All of us, both men and women, need a certain amount of social approval when it comes to our romantic choices. It's not at all uncommon to want everyone to think your boyfriend is the smartest, hottest, and most with-it guy in the room. So whether it's your friends' expectations or your parents wanting you to meet someone from the same background, it's hard to know where your list of demands begins and where theirs ends.

If you have hope of getting past your commitment issues, you'll have to stop trying to find the one guy who matches everyone's expectations. Your love life is not a democracy. Not everyone has to have an equal say. Remember, you're picky enough all on your own, so don't aggravate the situation by taking a public opinion poll after every date.

GET OVER IT: SUREFIRE STRATEGIES

"Yeah, yeah. So I'm picky! What else is new? But how do I stop being like this?" Good question. Admitting you have a problem is the first step. Say it with me: "I am a Nitpicker." Now that that's done with, you'll need a practical strategy for curbing your nitpicky ways. After all, it won't do you a bit of good if you don't have a plan. So if you're ready to stop picking *on* guys and start picking *out* the right one for you, read on to find answers to your prickliest Nitpicker dilemmas.

> **Q. "So okay, you may have a point. My list of require-ments is a little too long. But I really want all those qualities in a guy. What do I do?"**

A. To be fair, your shopping list doesn't have to be scrapped in its entirety. It probably contains some valid requirements that reflect your true affinities. The trouble for most Nit-pickers is figuring out what's important and what's not—what's a household item versus a luxury item. One way to separate the essentials from the nonessentials is to write a list of all your prerequisites. Notice that the qualities at the top of your list are more important than those at the bot-tom. Now take a look to see where you could compromise a little. Is it all that important that he be from the Midwest? Does he really need to sleep on the right side of the bed?

You should also pay careful attention to things that can be changed over time. If the guy you're with has bad table manners, dated duds, or an awful haircut, I'm sure you're savvy enough to help him change his ways. And if you have anything on your list that sounds like "nice car," "sculpted abs," or "cash/money," you may need to strike those off im-mediately. After all, the car may be leased, the abs may go in a few years, and the market can always plummet. Once you eliminate the extra, more trivial items, make sure you in-clude the non-negotiables—we're talking honesty, kindness, emotional maturity, and trustworthiness. You'd be surprised how many Nitpickers, with all their selectivity, forget to add these important and valuable traits to their lists.

THE DOCTOR IS IN

If you are having trouble committing, I think you really need to examine what your standards are, what the characteristics you are looking for are. And if you're happy with them, then you have to stand behind your choice. If, on the other hand, you look at those characteristics and decide that you really are being too unrealistic trying to find the perfect person, then you can change that and understand that the more stringent your requirements are, the fewer the people in the world who will be able to meet them. That's a mathematical truism.

—*Dr. Michael S. Broder*

EXERCISE: SHORT AND SWEET: THE NEW SHOPPING LIST

Here's your chance to bring your shopping list back down to a manageable size. Just follow the instructions to create a completely revamped list. Of course, even this new list should be used with a grain of salt. If you meet someone who doesn't fit all your criteria, don't rule them out just because of some "shopping list" you read about in a book.

Step 1: Rank each item on your shopping list according to importance.
Step 2: Find the top five items on your list and fill in the "must-haves" column.
Step 3: Find the next five highest-ranking items and enter into the "preferences" column.
Step 4: Find the last five items and enter these into the "luxury items" column.

MUST-HAVES	PREFERENCES	LUXURY ITEMS
1.	1.	1.
2.	2.	2.
3.	3.	3.

4.	4.	4.
5.	5.	5.

Note: When you're finished, you'll find that most of your "must-haves" will be general (e.g., trustworthy, good-hearted, adventurous, etc.), with "preferences" and "luxury items" becoming more specific (e.g., pet person, health nut, museum goer, etc.).

Q. *"I've always found that I get along much better with people when we have lots in common. I tried dating all kinds of men—business guys, firemen, and once a professor—but if they're too different, it always ends disastrously. What's so wrong with wanting someone to be more like me?"*

A. It's funny, but if you look at what a Nitpicker wants most, it's usually nearly a carbon copy of herself. Me! Me! Me!

- If I'm ambitious, I want someone as ambitious, if not more so.
- I have a quirky sense of humor, and so should he.
- I'm outgoing and like to party a lot, and I want someone just like me.

Okay, while having the major things in common is important, such as life goals and basic value systems, you don't want to end up with someone who's exactly like you. In fact, complementing each other is much more important. After all, can you imagine two high-energy people in one room together? They'd wear each other out. Or picture two ultra-ambitious people trying to raise a family together—it would leave much less opportunity for quality time together. Of course, there are some differences that can be tough to bridge. You're a Republican, he's a Democrat. Or you're a vegetarian, and he's a die-hard meat lover. But even these differences are surmountable, provided both of you are able to compromise and give each other room to be yourselves. So while it's great that you like yourself, differences can be healthy. After all, who couldn't use a little yin for their yang?

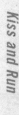

Q. *"It's funny—all my friends say I'm the pickiest person they know, but somehow, in the end, I manage to pick out the biggest losers. If I'm so picky, shouldn't I be ending up with better guys?"*

A. I get this question all the time. Would it make sense if I told you that you may be picky about the *wrong* things? Unless there's some serious instant attraction, Nitpickers will rarely give a guy a second chance. After all, it's all too easy to confuse hormones with compatibility. I've known very picky women who throw their carefully compiled lists right out the window upon meeting a guy who looks the part (basically, he's hot). A great personality? An astounding wit? Not even close. When you're sexually attracted to someone, it seems like they can do no wrong. But when you're not, the poor dear can recite lines from your favorite obscure French poet while standing on his head and still not make the cut. The question is: are your hormones doing a number on you and making that hot dud with an IQ of 60 seem like the best catch in town?

While some relationships start off with a bang, it takes much more than just chemistry to keep it going. In fact, the guys you're usually attracted to right away—smooth operators who are able to hook you with their charisma and charm—are usually not the best candidates for a relationship. No matter how you slice it, the majority of good relationships rarely start with two people lunging across the table at each other. Of course, there has to be some level of attraction, but if that is the deciding factor for a second or even a first date, you could start to wonder if you're being picky about the right things.

Even if you've already had great sex with someone, it's never too late to get your head back on straight. Ask yourself: "Would I enjoy spending time with my man stallion if we couldn't have sex? Would I still look forward to hanging out with him?" Also, when disqualifying men who aren't revving your engine, consider giving the chemistry more time to develop. The guy may be shy, worried about rushing into anything, or secure enough in himself not to have to put on a grand fireworks display during your first date. So if you don't feel sparks on day one, there's a good chance the second test drive might yield better results.

✚ THE DOCTOR IS IN

In our culture we're kind of trained to go for that falling-in-love experience. We are trained to look for the chemistry as a sign that this is the one for me. So a woman who is just essentially following the script that she has been socialized to follow might very well be behaving in this way. She might not be intentionally sabotaging herself, but she's being emotionally promiscuous. And there's an immaturity there. Most likely, she's falling in love with an illusion. As soon as the illusion is revealed to be what it is, she's on to the next one and not stopping to notice that something's not working here. And that's part of what maturity is: realizing after a while that I'm going for the chemistry. I'm dancing with an illusion here. This isn't working. If I want a committed relationship, I

Q. *"It's all well and good to tell me not to focus on his flaws. But when I'm on a date and notice something weird, like my last date who still carried a Velcro wallet, it's like 'Uh-oh!' And then I can't think about anything but that! What do I do?"*

A. I feel your pain. No one should have to see what you did. Velcro? Oh, the horror! In all seriousness, resisting the urge to pick apart, criticize, and analyze is much easier said than done; sometimes it even seems downright impossible. So how do you stop yourself from dissecting every man who crosses your path? Well, for starters, you'll have to put down that magnifying glass and try to put your inner Ebert on hiatus so you can really see the person in front of you. Instead of carefully scrutinizing every word, expression, or gesture, quiet your mind, suspend your judgment, and consider your feelings. That's right, *feelings*! Really tune in to yourself to find out how this guy makes you feel about you. Not the feeling you get about *him*, but how you feel about *yourself* when you're together. Are you confident? Do you find yourself holding back? Are you worried about making a good impression? Do you feel relaxed and able to be yourself? When all is said and done, these are the most important considerations.

Elina Furman

THE CONFESSIONAL: Cassy, 28

I met this one guy while walking home from work. Even though he was just okay-looking, I agreed to have coffee with him. The date wasn't what

Q. *"Look, I just don't have time to go on a gazillion dates to figure out if the guy is right for me. I work long hours as a financial analyst and barely have time to see the people I actually do like. It's either I'm into him or I'm not. One date is more than enough to know, isn't it?"*

A. In this crazy world of speed-dating parties, online dating, instant messaging, and triple booking, it's no wonder we've become so quick to dismiss guys. With more and more men floating by on love's conveyor belt, we begin to see them as one big hazy blur rather than the individuals they truly are. And since there are so many men out there and so little time to waste, we figure, "What's the point of going out with someone I don't want to see again?"

Take it from me, making rash decisions is one of the biggest mistakes Nitpickers make. When you meet someone you're on the fence about, it's not uncommon to refuse a second date. If there's even a shred of doubt about him, Nitpickers often end up chickening out and cutting off the relationship before it's even had a chance to begin. Believe me, I'm as guilty of that as anyone. And while living with ambiguity is tough, the best decision is often to make no decision at all.

"So how many dates exactly do I have to go on?" you ask. Well, in the end, it's really your call. There's no hard-

and-fast rule when it comes to these things. If the prospect of a second date is about as exciting as a trip to the dentist, it may not be such a good idea to accept. But if you're ambivalent or just don't care one way or another, you may want to try for a second or even a third date, depending on how things go. Who knows—if you just chill out for a minute, you may find that you have a lot in common. You may even get a new friend out of it (or at the very least, a free dinner).

NITPICKER RECAP

Okay, time's up. Put down your pencils. In the interest of our ADD, sound-bite culture, here's a quick recap of what you may have missed while you were too busy picking apart this chapter.

- No matter how specific your list of criteria is, you just can't order up a man like you would dinner take-out.

- You're great! We get it. But what could you possibly learn from dating a male clone of yourself?

- There's a difference between "must-haves" and "luxury items." Learn it, love it!

- Everyone is perfect when they are alone. It's when we decide to commit to someone that we finally realize we're far from it.

- Never forget the Blemish Bylaw: if you look, you shall find.

- If you don't feel sparks on date one, the second test drive might yield better results.

- You're picky enough as it is. Don't aggravate the situation by taking a public opinion poll after every date.

- And finally, if you're still waiting for that perfect guy to come along, take a seat. We're going to be here a while.

4

The Serial Dater

When I moved to Chicago from a small town in Indiana, I was floored. It was men, men, and more men. And they were all hot, interesting, smart, and some of them were even rich. Back home, the only available guy I knew was the 52-year-old mailman, who was rumored to have been dating three women in town, so suffice it to say my options were limited. Living in the city, I must have gone on at least four dates a week. I dated a guy who owned his own construction company, a fireman who wanted me to meet his mother after two dates, an underwear model, and even my doorman's cousin. And that's just the first month. I went on like this for a couple of years, dating A–Z, until I realized one day, after a bad breakup, that the whole thing was getting kind of tired. I was exhausted! I had not made any new girlfriends at all and never had time for myself. But every time I tried to slow down and stop dating, I would just meet someone new and off I went again.

It all starts innocently enough. You log on to Match.com to check out this crazy new invention called online dating. Next thing you know, you're juggling men, coming up with your own dating rules and acronyms (e.g., DWNK: divorced with no kids), and trying to figure out whether it was Matt or Matthew who hated sushi.

There's no telling when the serial dating bug can strike. You may be just getting out of a serious relationship, marriage, or long dry spell. But one thing's for certain: when it does it can become a really hard habit to break. All of a sudden, you find yourself addicted to love—at least the serial kind.

To be fair, it's extremely easy to fall into the serial dating mode.

After all, there's nothing like the adrenaline rush you feel when you're first getting to know someone. You know, that phase when he can say or do no wrong. So is it any wonder that many couples often talk about the "magic" of those first days and are constantly trying to recapture the glow? Well, Serial Daters take it one step further. They're so in love with love that they're constantly trying to re-create those magical feelings by dating new people. Many of the women I've interviewed find that they have become dating junkies or what's commonly known as "hyperdaters," where they set up ten online dates each week and even go on several dates in one night.

The Serial Dater is someone who juggles multiple partners and/or jumps from one short-lived (a week to three months) relationship to the next. She is never without a boyfriend and has never actually spent time on her own. She craves companionship but bolts at the first sign that something may be getting more serious. In fact, the Serial Dater usually suffers from the "grass-is-always-greener syndrome." Often she won't leave a relationship until she has set up another opportunity elsewhere, going from the arms of one lover to the next. So whatever your personal variation on the serial dating theme is, rest assured, you are definitely one of the most common breed of commitment-phobes.

You may be wondering how someone who's always got a man around can be a commitment-phobe. Well, it's simple. While Serial Daters are good at the short haul, long-term commitment isn't really their cup of java. Ultimately, the Serial Dater is scared to be alone, claims to want to be in a committed relationship, but can never stay with one partner for too long. By entering into short relationships, she can avoid facing both her fear of solitude and her fear of intimacy. When it comes to a real relationship, Serial Daters are simply not the sticking type. As soon as the thrill of the chase is gone, so are they.

For me, the serial dating journey began right after my ex-boyfriend and I broke up. One day, after seven years of dating one person in my twenties, I was free to pursue anyone I wanted. And that's exactly what I did, launching myself on a crazy dating spree that could rival Don Juan's. While some gents never made it to the two-date mark, a few lasted an epic three months. But as soon as things started to get serious, there I was saying something horribly obnoxious, avoiding phone calls, and deleting phone numbers. I remember one day scrolling through the list of names in my phone book, and I literally had no idea who half of the guys were. That's when I knew it was time for a break.

Looking back, I realize that serial dating filled a huge gap in my life. Not only did I feel a bit lonely and empty after the breakup, but having all those guys around to compliment me was highly addictive. Of course, now I realize that taking a break from dating would have been the best thing for me, but I was too anxious to get out there to see what I had been missing. I was too eager to find out how I measured up in the new dating market and would have done anything to avoid thinking about the ex—or about myself, for that matter.

The problem with serial dating is that it can distract you from important things, such as getting to know yourself, creating stronger friendships, and really learning about the people you're with. What with all those hours you spend doing your hair, finding the perfect pair of shoes, and coming up with scintillating anecdotes, just imagine how much time you'd have to devote to solving some of the world's problems—or, at the very least, some of your own. In the end, I highly doubt that serial dating is the way of the future. Dating shouldn't be like rifling through the bargain bin until you find something worthy, only to return it months later when you spot the defect. No matter how tempting it is to start over with someone new again and again, there's definitely emotional fallout to staying on the dating merry-go-round long after the park has closed.

THE DOCTOR IS IN

Serial dating can be very exciting. You can fly off to the Bahamas with some rich banker guy for the weekend. It's always wanting that rush of the first kiss, that first weekend you spent in bed naked. The thrill of the new romance can be addictive. The mundane real world of being in a married relationship is not flying off to the Bahamas, but it is know-ing your husband, your partner more deeply than anybody else in the world. The first stage of any relationship is very heady and exciting. And if you are addicted to that, you don't have a sense that there is an excitement to getting to know someone and sharing yourself with someone on a deep level. That can be thrilling, too, but in a different, more grounded, calmer, and deeper way.

—*Allison Moir-Smith, M.A.*

QUIZ: ARE YOU A SERIAL DATER?

Think you're exempt from the serial dating category? Well, there's only one sure way to find out. After all, we're all guilty of serial dating at some point in our lives. So whether you're proud of your dating prowess or are convinced you don't have one serial bone in your body, take this quiz to find out where you fall on the serial dating meter.

1. **You've been dating someone for about two months and are get-ting bored. You:**
   A. Reactivate your online profile without telling him.
   B. Tell him you want to start seeing other people.
   C. Plan fun activities to bring back the spark, such as cooking or salsa dance classes.

2. **How did you handle your last breakup?**
   A. Stopped calling. It's not like you were committed or anything.
   B. Sent him a stock e-mail response that reads, "You're really great, I'm just not ready for anything serious right now."
   C. Had a long talk and you both agreed it would be better to end it.

3. **How many online dating sites are you currently a member of?**
   A. 4 or more
   B. 2–3
   C. 0–1

4. Your best friend just announced she's getting married and you're in the wedding party. Your biggest concern is:

A. Whom to take as my date. I don't want any of my boyfriends to think the wedding invite means we're getting serious.

B. Girls' night out. Now I'll need to find a new gal pal to go out on the town with.

C. Whether I can lose enough weight to fit into the bridesmaid's dress.

5. You've just come home after a stressful day of work. What do you do?

A. Check out the Craigslist "missed connections" page to see if that hottie in the elevator posted a note for me.

B. Check my e-mail and return phone calls.

C. Pour myself a glass of wine and take a long hot bath.

6. You're on a date with a guy you met online and it's going terribly. He looks nothing like the photo he sent and he lied about his age. What do you do?

A. No sweat. I already called my friend and she's bailing me out in . . . Oh, that's her calling now.

B. Spend an hour chatting and then pretend I have an early meeting in the morning.

C. Grin and bear it.

7. What's your favorite thing about dating in general?

A. Free dinners and tickets to shows.

B. Meeting tons of cool new people I'd never get to know otherwise.

C. Learning about what I like and don't like.

8. If you were to look through your phone contacts right now, how many numbers belong to guys you've dated at some point in your life?

A. 11 or more

B. 6–10

C. 0–5

9. **This hot new guy you met at the health club invites you to opera in the park on Thursday. But you also have another date planned with the guy you've been seeing for a month. What do you do?**

A. Double-book. Early drinks with your current guy, followed by a night of music under the stars with the new one.

B. Postpone the new guy until Friday night. He can wait.

C. Say no to the new guy. After all, you're already seeing someone else.

10. **You gave your phone number to someone you met at a lounge. When he calls you two weeks later, you:**

A. Schedule him in for a dinner—three weeks from now.

B. Tell him you'll need to check your schedule, but then accept the date. He *was* really cute.

C. Take a pass. Anyone who waits that long to call must be a player.

Scoring: To calculate your final score, assign a point value to each answer: 3 for every A, 2 for every B, and 1 for every C. Now add it all up to see where you stand!

23–30 Points: Seriously Serial

Look up "serial dater" in the dictionary and you'll probably find your picture. When it comes to doing the dating rounds, you've probably done them all. While I would never begrudge a gal her wining and dining, you really should consider slowing down a bit. After all, you wouldn't want to be labeled a dating junkie, would you? While staying cool and casual can be fun for a while, it couldn't hurt to get to know some of these guys beyond their first names and job descriptions.

15–22 Points: Playing the Field

When it comes to dating, you're no slouch. You've been there and done that, and are proud to say you've met your share of interesting matches. Since you definitely exhibit some serial dating tendencies, you should take the above advice and work on your *relating* and not just your *dating* skills. Translation: Try dating one person at a time, take the time to really get to know him, and let your guard down once in a while so that he can return the favor.

14 or Fewer Points: Looking Good

While no one would call you an amateur in the dating department, you're definitely not a pro, either. That's a good thing! You would never think of treating dating as a game, and you realize that people are far more complex than their first impressions. Good for you. While building a relationship takes time and hard work, you're on the right track.

SERIAL DATER PROTESTS: "I'M NOT A SERIAL DATER, I JUST . . ."

Excuses, excuses! There are a million and one ways to rationalize serial dating. After all, it's not like you're hurting anyone, save for the poor schmuck you've bumped off the schedule three weeks in a row. And it's not like you're the only serial offender out there, what with all your friends rotating men faster than their day-of-the-week underwear. So whether you've admitted to being a Serial Dater, couldn't care less, or are insulted at the very insinuation, read on to find out if yours are among the most common protests.

1. **"I Just Like Variety."** Oh yes, the old variety-is-the-spice-of-life routine. Of course, men have been getting away with it for eons. You know, the ones who claim to love women, all women. So isn't it about time that we girls return the compliment? It's fair to say that Serial Daters just can't get enough Y chromosome in their diet. Ask them to pick just one male specimen or even (gasp!) take a one-week break from dating, and they'll combust on the spot from the sheer effort. Does your schedule read anything like this?

   - Tuesday: Poetry reading with Dan, the banker
   - Wednesday: Salsa dancing with Rich, the actor
   - Friday: Loft/rooftop party with DJ Andy
   - Saturday: Pistons game with Kyle, the lawyer

   If so, you definitely have a high variety tolerance and are able to mix it up and enjoy yourself in any setting. Serial dating is great for people who want to play up different parts of their personality. You can play out your glamorous side with a

Euro buttoned-up type one night and then go boho chic with an artsy musician type the next. But trying on men isn't like changing your outfit!

While you may pride yourself on your always-changing chameleon ways, you can also end up overdoing it and spreading yourself too thin. Can anyone say "identity crisis"? Trying on a different man for size every night may seem like good clean, harmless fun at first. But in the end, it can also leave you confused, anxious, and struggling to find out who you are and what you really want.

THE CONFESSIONAL: Kylie, 34

Ever since I hit puberty, I've been accused of being boy-crazy. And I guess that would be about right. I've dated more than 150 guys and am still counting. Problem is, I'm dying to meet someone I really like. But somehow it never works out. It's not that I'm picky; I just don't have good luck choosing men. Sometimes, right after a breakup, I start to feel like I'm going crazy and panic, like "Who am I going to have Chinese take-out with?" or "Who's going to call me to say good night?" It's almost like a physical reaction, like this huge hole has opened up and I have to fill it—fast! Then I go out to avoid the misery, and that's when I meet someone again. It just goes on and on like this. It's sad, but looking back, I realize I've never spent more than two weeks alone. I really want to find that one person I really like, whom I can trust and be with for a while, but it never works out for me.

2. **"I Just Don't Like to be Alone."** Well, who does? For all that talk about solitude building character, making you stronger, and yada-yada-yada, sometimes you just can't take another minute of it. Sometimes you just want to cuddle up next to someone—even if you did just meet them at the corner deli.

Loneliness is an undeniable part of being single. If it wasn't for our collective fear of ending up alone, sick, and unloved, then there wouldn't be a dating or self-help industry, period. We all fill up our days with distractions and activities—calling our friends, checking our e-mail, texting our latest crush—anything and everything to avoid sitting still for a minute. Ask any single person if she gets lonely, and then watch her lie through her teeth. No one's saying you don't have plenty of friends, family, and coworkers to keep you entertained, but that doesn't mean you don't crave romantic companionship from time to time.

Well, for a little while, at least. But once you've had your fix, it's not uncommon to do a complete 180, wanting nothing more than the option of a long, uninterrupted day without a man in sight. And that's the problem. While many of you Serial Daters hate to be alone and need to have a variety of men on speed dial, you also hate feeling obligated to be with someone. For all your talk about not wanting to be alone, you have to admit that sometimes you wouldn't have it any other way. And that's why it's so hard to maintain a relationship. You want someone to be there for you, but you would prefer to dictate all the terms, like when, where, and how long they should stick around.

3. **"I Just Got Out of a Relationship."** What with your ego bruised and all those Kleenex-filled nights spent ranting about how you were done with him anyway, it's no wonder you're looking for a little male affection. No matter who broke up with whom, ending a relationship is always a miserable, humbling experience. On one hand, you're dying to start mingling and see if your dating stock is still high. On the other, you haven't fully recovered and spend most of your time staring at your date's Treo 650 because it's the same one your ex had. Many of us believe that the best way to get over someone is to start dating right away. After all, not only can meeting a new guy make you forget all about that ex, it's also a confidence booster when you're down for the count. And since the last thing you want is to get involved with someone seriously, why not keep your options open and date casually for a while, right?

While I would never advise anyone to languish after a breakup, running into the fire pit too fast can cause all sorts of unnecessary complications. Look, we've all been there. We've either dated someone on the rebound or broken someone's heart while trying to mend our own. Either way, it's not a good idea to start circulating too soon. Rebound dating inevitably leads to meeting all the wrong men, which in turn can make you more commitment-phobic in the long run.

Instead of dating as a means to distract yourself, take a break and spend some time pondering your role in the breakup. Yes, no matter how innocent you think you were in the affair, it always takes two people to drive the final nail into the coffin. Was it poor judgment? Irreconcilable differences? Was it your own fear of commitment that did the relationship in? Not to suggest that you spend all your time berating yourself, but a little introspection never hurt anyone. Then, when you're ready to meet someone new, you'll have learned from your mistakes, recovered sufficiently, and may even be able to take the new relationship past the one-month mark.

THE CONFESSIONAL: Kim, 30

Actually, it was about a year ago that I decided to date several people at the same time. It wasn't something I had done before. I was coming out of a long relationship. I decided I wasn't ready to get back into a relationship. I actually met somebody I really liked fairly quickly on. But I was afraid that that person might be a rebound. I felt he was too good to be a rebound, so I figured I could insulate him from being a possible rebound by going out with other people. And also, I sort of wanted to look around and see who else was out there. I think he accepted that and he, too, wasn't ready to make a commitment. So I don't think it was problematic. I think the main issue that arises is spreading yourself too thin when you are dating multiple people because invariably there's going to be one person you like more than the rest. It's hard to manage from an emotional perspective and from a logistical perspective. Just even from the standpoint of not having enough time to devote to the people in your life or the new people that come in. It's also difficult to manage because no matter how much people tell you that they are not jealous, those feelings tend to surface eventually.

Celeb Serial Daters

When it comes to playing musical dating chairs, these Hollywood divas wrote the book. These leading ladies are proof positive than when you're young, gorgeous, and in demand, it's all too easy to fall into serial dating mode.

Scarlett Johansson. The über-glam star of such films as *The Nanny Diaries* and *Lost in Translation* is young, powerful, and beautiful—and she knows it. This is one saucy chick that is in her prime, so who are we to try to curb her serial dating ways? She's hooked up with all kinds of scrumptious male leads, including Benicio del Toro, Jared Leto, Heath Ledger, and Josh Hartnett—and who could blame her? If her record-breaking schedule of back-to-back movies is any indicator of her love life, then prepare to hear a lot more about her exploits in the near future.

Paris Hilton. Leave it to Ms. Hilton to take this serial dating thing to a whole new level. In fact, Paris represent a very unique type of Serial Dater, the kind of girl who makes out with a guy once and then (oops!) somehow she's in yet another relationship. While some girls can kiss a billion frogs, Paris somehow ends up dating every one of them—think notorious exes Rick Solomon and Fred Durst.

Winona Ryder. Matt Damon, Johnny Depp, David Duchovny, Christian Slater, Daniel Day-Lewis, Beck, Peter Yorn, Jimmy Fallon, Ryan Adams—the list does go on. With an impressive list of hotties under her belt, Winona can be forgiven her shopping indiscretion a few years back. What with all those hot dates, it's no wonder she needed so many cute outfits.

Drew Barrymore. The talented and beautiful actress/producer of such films as *Happily Ever After, Charlie's Angels,* and *Lucky You* is one of Hollywood's most lovable serial daters. She's been linked to every lead actor under the sun and has three marriages under her belt at the ripe old age of 34. But don't hate her 'cause she's serial. When you're as cute and down-to-earth as she is, it's hard to get away from those throngs of male admirers.

TOP SERIAL DATER HANG-UPS

When it comes to serial dating, it's all too easy to dismiss the topic with a quick wave of the hand. After all, why should everyone else get to have all the fun? If you can't beat them, why not join them, right? Okay, while you are in fact normal and just doing what everyone expects of you as the fabulous, single girl that you are, the question you have to ask yourself is whether you're really happy. Can you honestly say that engaging in a string of brief, casual relationships will ultimately be more fulfilling than committing yourself to just one? If you answered yes, do not pass go and proceed directly to your next date (he's probably already waiting at the bar). If not, stick around and check out some of the most common Serial Dater mishaps.

1. More, More, More!

Meet a hundred people and one of them is bound to be your Mr. Right, no? Like the old adage goes, you have to kiss lots of frogs to find your prince. But do you really? In our hurry-afflicted, quantity-over-quality drive-through society, there's speed dating, group dinner dates, online dating, and all kinds of other attempts made by dating companies to part you and your hard-earned money. After all, there's a reason all those organizations are telling you that dating is a numbers game. They want you to pay for the privilege of playing again . . . and again . . . and again. And the more you date, the more these companies make. Sure, you've met a lot of interesting people, like that professional comedian who laughs at his own fart jokes or that accountant who asked you to cut up his meat for him, but can you really say you've met that many quality people?

If you find yourself saying, "I'm not a Serial Dater, I'm just proactive about finding 'the one,'" stop and really think about what you're doing. The idea that dating more people will help you find "the one" is downright ridiculous. If that were the case, the reality shows *The Bachelor* and *The Bachelorette* would be yielding much better results. And while I'm not suggesting that you spend every night sitting around watching *Newlyweds* reruns ('cause we all know how Jessica and Nick's story turned out), there is such a thing as overresearching your options. When it's all about the next guy, the next conquest, and the next dinner, you tend to lose interest in the idea of dating just one person and may pass up someone great in the process. Let's face it—no matter how perfect he is, there's no single guy on earth who can compete with a gaggle of attractive suitors.

2. Defensive Dating

How many times have you strung a guy along (let's call him the substitute boyfriend) knowing full well you weren't that into him, just to have backup plans in case the guy you really liked failed to call on time? We've all done it, so go ahead and admit it. Juggling lots of men can seem like an empowering move—at first. You figure, "Well, the guys are probably doing the same thing, so why can't I?" But in the end, the juggling act is really just a manifestation of what I call defensive dating.

Defensive dating isn't really about empowerment, it's about fear. You're afraid that someone might break up with you, so you have three other guys waiting in the wings. You're afraid your boyfriend is cheating on you, so you figure you'll be emotionally covered if you do the same. You're afraid that if you date only one person, you will become a needy, dependent stalker, following him home after work every night. You have so much fear that you avoid committing to any one person, just in case he ends up disappointing you.

Juggling lots of men may seem like the best way to curb all your doubts, anxieties, and insecurities, but it just ends up creating more problems in the long run. Not only do you end up wasting lots of time dating backup guys you don't even really like, it can backfire if you're not up-front with your dates. So when in doubt, and as hard as it is, make an effort to date one person at a time. It may not be the modern thing to do (okay, it may even seem downright archaic), but it sure beats ruining a perfectly good relationship before it's even had the chance to bloom.

THE CONFESSIONAL: Michelle, 27

I am definitely guilty of dating more than one guy a time. A lot of times they will even be at the same place and I'll have to go back and forth between the two all night without them knowing it. Last week it blew up in my face, though, because I had no idea the guys were fraternity brothers once upon a time and still good friends. Oops! But the way I figure it, if you're going to settle for someone that's not an absolute fit for you, you might as well get everything you want in several different people. Also, guys are great at letting you down, and when they do, you don't feel as bad when you have someone else to fall back on.

3. The Preemptive Strike

It's a cardinal rule of Dating 101: never let anyone break up with you first, especially if it's someone you don't even like all that much. Imagine the humiliation of being broken up with by someone who wasn't even worthy of you to begin with.

Admit it—you've done this before. Think someone is about to break up with you? Then beat them to the punch and sack them instead. It's as easy as 1-2-3, and most Serial Daters have the preemptive breakup move down cold. They know all the signs of an oncoming breakup and are always watching to see when their guy is about to strike the blow. Big things like not returning calls in ten minutes, making reservations at the wrong restaurant, and going out of town on a last-minute business trip are all definite indicators that he's planning to give you the boot—well, at least to Serial Daters they are.

For many serial offenders, dating is purely a game, and the object is to break up with them before you get broken up with. It's that simple. But what if you're wrong? What if your paranoia is doing a number on you and that perfectly nice guy who you think is about to break your heart has no intention of doing any such thing? So consider yourself warned: the next time you feel yourself getting trigger-happy, remember that you may very well be breaking up with a great guy who is, in fact, really into you.

And while you may win the breakup game, you may lose something much more important in the process.

4. Slim Pickings

Many Serial Daters date too much because they feel there's just not enough men to go around. Think about it. How many times have you or your friends said, "There are just no men"? No, really—I can't walk one single block without hearing some variation of this ubiquitous single woman's mantra. And while it may be the common consensus, it couldn't be further from the truth. Despite what we've been told about the so-called man shortage, the U.S. Census Bureau has reported a surplus of 80,000 thirty-something men for every million women of the same age. Furthermore, by 2010, men aged 35 to 44 will outnumber women ages 30 to 34 by two to one. That gives you twice the odds of meeting someone great.

Even with all the evidence to the contrary and the fact that they've been on a date every night since the prom, some Serial Daters are convinced that there's a scarcity of males and end up accepting a date with any Tom, Dick, or Harry who comes along. While the Nitpicker type is too selective, Serial Daters are often not picky enough and often don't take the time to adequately screen their dates. After all, it's hard to say no when every date could possibly be your last.

So what am I proposing that Serial Daters do? Be more picky. After all, if you go out with every guy you meet, the quantity may go up, but the quality of your interactions may diminish. In the end, it may be great to feel popular, in demand, and desired by the opposite sex, but if you think every date is the equivalent of the Last Supper, you may end up overstuffed and emotionally undernourished.

5. Act 1, Scene 3,000

It should come as no surprise that Serial Daters thrive on attention and delivering a good performance. In fact, all of us, women and men, have a dating persona that we bring to the table—you know, that stock supply of quirky stories, jokes, and flirty maneuvers. There's something so thrilling about having a captive or, at the very least, cute audience hanging on your every word. Besides your psychologist, mom, and best friend, there are few people who would sit still while you recount all your exploits in full detail. I don't know what it is, but there's just this charge that makes you want to be funnier and more talkative on a date. It's like you, but better—version 10.0.

I can't claim to be exempt. In my two years of doing the dating rounds, I milked my "dating expert" status for all it was worth. Every guy would automatically assume I was this Carrie Bradshaw type, always going to parties and living an ultra-exciting lifestyle. And while some would furrow their brow at the thought that I was writing about our dates, most were excited by the challenge. Needless to say, I didn't want to disappoint. There was just something very glamorous about the persona I adopted. More importantly, it was also very protective. There was never a chance that they would get to know who I really was, and at the time that was just fine by me.

Serial Daters tend to rely on their dating persona to the point where they really begin to believe they're as captivating as they make themselves sound. But that's the problem: once you're all out of material, you want to find a new guy who's never heard your spiel before. Like a camera-hungry actress who's always ready for her next close-up, you're addicted to the challenge of performing, not relating. But as fun as it is, the dating persona is just that—a persona. Not only is it extremely superficial, it's not who you are. In fact, having a dating persona is a great way to avoid commitment, since it prevents people from achieving true intimacy and finding out about each other.

WHEN THE GRASS IS *NOT* GREENER

Awww! You're in love. You're spending every night at his place, sharing childhood memories, and may even have bought an extra toothbrush in a moment of extreme fidelity. But after a few weeks or even months, you find yourself getting a little bored. He's great and all, but . . . well, you know. So you start scrolling through the online dating ads just to see what you're missing, and you start thinking, "Hmmm . . . maybe I can do even better." Or you're out with your friends when you notice a hottie in the corner and start wondering what he looks like in his boxer briefs. At some point, no matter how much in love, we all have a tendency to wonder what it would be like to wander.

1. **We always want what we can't have.** When you're dating, you can't help but drool over every cute guy who crosses your path. But as much as you don't like to think about it, one of the main reasons they're attracted to you is precisely because you're taken. Believe me, there's nothing more alluring about a man or woman than the aura of unavailability. Just remember that if you were single, you probably wouldn't date half of them, nor would they date you.

2. **Don't comparison-shop.** If you're happy with your guy and are trying to make a go of it, resist the urge to browse online sites to see what else is out there. It might seem like a harmless way to spend a Sunday afternoon, but it only adds fuel to your commitment-phobia. After all, if you've been looking to date a Fortune 500 CEO at the top of the power list and actually start dating him, there still might be a cuter one next year who ranks even higher. Moral of the story? No matter what your criteria, there's always going to be someone who matches it better.

3. **Water your own damn grass.** Looking on the other side of the fence means you're not paying attention to your own relationship. Start by doing little things to keep the union fun and exciting, and pretty soon you'll be saying, "What grass?"

4. **Don't look over your shoulder.** If you're with your guy, give him your undivided attention. Acting like the poster girl for ADD and flirting with other guys won't make you seem happier, vied after, or confident, just egotistical and vain.

THE DOCTOR IS IN

It's important to be realistic about what you can expect from a partner and what you can actually contribute in a relationship. A lot of times there's a great beginning, a great start. But once the relationship starts to get serious and we're called upon to deal with conflicts and issues, that's where the commitment-phobia is going to rear its ugly head.

—Debra Mandel, Ph.D.

GET OVER IT: SUREFIRE STRATEGIES

While it's great that you're socializing, learning you shouldn't eat spicy food after midnight, and discovering that dating 21-year-old models is not as fun as it used to be, many of you are still pressuring yourselves to get out there and mingle. Believe me, I've been there and I know how strong the pressure can be. But let's get one thing straight: dating burnout is not a myth. And while there's no magic button that will rid you of the serial dating virus overnight, check out some tips for doing just that.

Q. *"Maybe I'm missing something here. How can I be commitment-phobic if I'm always looking for someone to settle down with? It's not like I date a lot because I enjoy it. I just want to increase my chances. It's not my fault I never meet the right guy, but that doesn't mean I should stop trying, right?"*

A. I totally get where you're coming from. It does seem kind of counterintuitive. After all, if you were really commitment-phobic, you'd be sitting at home organizing your sock drawer every night or spending all your time poring over the latest financial reports at work, right? But as we all know, nothing in life is ever this simple. There are many ways to avoid commitment. Some of us never date at all,

Elina Furman

which is one surefire way to avoid meeting someone, while others spend all their time in dead-end relationships. And still, there are others like you, my brave Serial Daters, who spend all your time chasing and pursuing dates rather than taking some time to figure out what it is you're really after.

While you may be going on a gazillion dates because you think it will increase your chances of meeting the right guy, you may be stopping yourself from achieving the very goal you're after. If you're always exhausted and exasperated by the mad hunt for that elusive Mr. Right, you're probably in no condition to recognize him even if he did materialize. And even if he did come along, he might not recognize you as Mrs. Right, either. After all, I'm sure his idea of Mrs. Right isn't someone who's dating three other guys at the same time and subscribes to every dating service in town.

Q. *"You're acting like this is all my fault, like I'm the one who goes after all these guys. But is it my fault that men really like me? And what's so wrong with dating so many men anyway? I love the attention and it makes me feel really good about myself."*

A. For all I know, you may very well be God's gift to men, able to drive an arrow into any man's heart just by passing him on the street. And while you may be completely innocent and would never consciously flirt with anyone, isn't there something to say for personal accountability? I mean, just because someone asks you out, do you automatically have to say yes?

I always say that the best thing about dating is "so many men, so many compliments." Dating can be a great way to boost your confidence, especially if you've recently lost weight, ended a relationship, or moved to a new city. And while it's great to feel vied after, it's too easy to lead men on and give them false hope when all you're looking for is an ego boost. By viewing men as nothing more than quick pick-me-ups, you'll be doing yourself a disservice in the long run. Eventually, you'll forget how to give yourself internal reinforcement and will come to depend on the good opinion of others. And isn't the most attractive type of person someone who doesn't need constant attention and reinforcement?

In the end, if you find yourself dating for superficial reasons, you will end up meeting superficial people. It's just that simple. Once you take the ego out of dating, you can begin to think about what a commitment could bring to your life. You may even find yourself dating a higher caliber of men who would never put up with such high-maintenance foolishness. And while the guy you end up with may not spend every waking minute telling you how great your butt looks in those pants, you might find out that the rewards outweigh this one minor drawback.

Q. *"Lately, I've been going out on all these dates, and sometimes I just want to scream. If I have to tell one more person about my job at the vet clinic, my crazy family, or my entire relationship history, I swear I'm going to move to Alaska. What should I do?"*

A. First of all, take a deep breath. What we have here are the classic symptoms of dating burnout. And it's no wonder. You've probably overtaxed yourself by attending every party, lecture, and open bar in a five-mile radius. Of course you're tired, cranky, and annoyed. Who wouldn't be? Here are some of the most common signs of dating burnout.

- You've started bringing a list of questions on every date to speed up the getting-to-know-you process.
- You're having a hard time keeping track of whom you're supposed to meet when.
- You've called the guy you're dating by the wrong name on three different occasions.
- You find yourself not wanting to go anywhere, and have

to be dragged out of the house by your concerned girl-friends.

- You keep track of all the people you're dating by keeping a list of names with a description of what they look like.
- You lose your temper over minor things, such as a date showing up five minutes late.
- You fantasize about moving to a foreign country where you don't speak the language so you can stop dating altogether.

If you've experienced three or more of the above symptoms, you may indeed be suffering from dating burnout. The first thing you should ask yourself is why you're dating so much in the first place. Is it that you're ready to meet someone or you worry that if you don't go out you might miss your one chance to meet Mr. Perfect, who is probably at the party right now?

Granted, there is immense social pressure to go out, but a little break now and then is good for you. It's the same with your career. Too many long nights at the office with too little reward can turn any self-starter into a disgruntled worker. But remember, dating shouldn't be a job. If you overdo it in the dating department, you may just find yourself feeling listless, uninspired, and anything but ready for love.

 THE CONFESSIONAL: Natalie, 36

I'm kind of an attractive woman and guys end up liking me, so I tend to get paired up with someone. I think I need to spend more time alone, not to distract myself with dating. So no dating, at least for a few more weeks or months. I need to work through all this, and then hopefully after I do a little more work on myself I will draw the right kind of man into my life. My goal is to be able to participate in the relationship 100 percent and not for it to be all about me. I'm going to have to have a stronger identity, because that's what I'm struggling with. I am a big advocate of taking an honest look at yourself.

Q. *"So you want me to stop dating altogether? Are you crazy?"*

A. While it may seem radical or even downright insane at first, I firmly believe that taking a good old-fashioned dating sabbatical now and then can be just what the doctor ordered. Let's call it a "dating detox." And don't pout! While I realize this won't make me the most popular dating guru in town, I wouldn't say it if I didn't think it was time to implement some drastic measures. Taking a dating break can reconnect you with yourself and help you redefine what it is you're looking for. Think of it as recharging your dating batteries. After all, spending all your time running from the arms of one man to another has probably made you lose touch with why you're dating in the first place. Is it to meet the right guy you can spend the rest of your life with? Is it to have someone to hang with when you're bored? Is it finding someone to buy you nice presents? Or is it to appease all those critics who are constantly telling you to get out there?

All of us date for different reasons, and those reasons are bound to change over time. While we've all suffered from dating delirium at some point in our lives, a dating fast can be a great way to realign your outlook. After all, filling up all your time with dead-end dates can keep you from achieving your goal of finding the person who is right for you. Still not convinced? Here are some other benefits of a dating detox that may win you over.

- **Swinging Solo.** While no one prefers to be alone, you have to admit it's not the end of the world, either. But isn't being alone better than staying on the merry-go-round of short, unfulfilling relationships? One of the best things that a dating detox can provide is a reminder of the joys of being single. God knows you need it. In the end, learning to like your own company will make

Elina Furman

you much more commitment-friendly when you are ready to stop and be with one person for a change. When it comes to spending quality time on your own, practice really does make perfect. And remember, solitude is not being alone, it's time spent with your favorite person—you.

- **Getting Real.** What with every dating expert telling you to "brand" yourself in the marketplace so you can auction yourself off to the highest bidder, you're probably tired of treating every encounter like a Hollywood pitch meeting. A dating sabbatical is a great way to cut out all that ridiculousness from your life and start getting real—with yourself and the people you're meeting. Even if you just limit your dating ration to once a week or once every two weeks, you can start focusing on being yourself rather than trying to impress someone you don't even know if you like in the first place. Start by letting down your guard, taking time to ask serious questions of your dates, and really thinking about your responses without trying to present some hyperfascinating version of yourself. The quantity of your interactions may go down, but the quality is bound to improve.

- **So Many Men.** Not only can dating overdrive make you crazy, it can also prevent you from making sound decisions about the men in your life. Some of you probably have a skewed perception of guys, seeing them as caricatures rather than living, breathing people who continue to exist once you've kissed them goodbye at the door. Keeping men on permanent rotation may amuse you for a while, but isn't it time you stopped objectifying men? I mean, it's hard enough to keep all their names straight, let alone figure out if the guy in front of you is kind, loyal, and willing to bring you chicken soup when you're sick.

SERIAL DATER RECAP

Before you go rushing off on yet another dating adventure, take a minute to review this Serial Dater recap.

- It's important that you try to get to know your dates beyond their first names and job descriptions.

- Juggling lots of men isn't empowering, it's defensive.

- It's great to feel popular and desired, but if you think every date is the equivalent of the Last Supper, you may end up overstuffed and emotionally undernourished.

- The next time you plan a preemptive breakup, remember that you may very well be breaking up with a great guy who is, in fact, really into you.

- No matter what your dating criteria, there's always going to be someone out there who matches it better.

- If you find yourself dating for superficial reasons, you will end up meeting superficial people.

- Acting like the poster girl for ADD and flirting with other guys while on a date won't make you seem happier, vied after, or confident—you'll just come across as egotistical and vain.

- Not only is a dating persona extremely superficial, it's not who you are.

- If you're always exhausted by the mad hunt for that elusive Mr. Right, you'll be in no condition to recognize him when he does materialize.

- Taking a dating sabbatical can help you recharge your dating batteries and redefine what you're looking for.

5

The Tinker Bell

Lara's Story. I've been dating a guy for over a year now and he claims he's very in love with me. Problem is, he's married. I know! But he promised that he's going to get a divorce soon and wants to move in together. Of course, he's been saying it for months, so I don't know if he's serious.

Shannon's Story. I met this awesome guy at a club six months ago and we've been hooking up ever since. He's really great. I can tell him pretty much anything and we even have the same taste in movies, which is weird since I only like chick flicks. A couple of weeks ago I told him I wanted to be exclusive. In response he got really upset and told me he's not ready to be with one person. All my friends told me to break up with him, but I don't know. I really like him and we have so much fun when we're together.

Jessica's Story. I've been with this guy on and off for about three years now. He's had problems with drinking and drugs in the past and has cheated on me several times. But now I think I'm ready to get more serious. The lease on my apartment is running out and I proposed that we move in together. Well, that didn't go over too well. He freaked out and accused me of pushing him too hard. Maybe he's right.

Pop quiz: What do all these women have in common?

   A. They're all dating commitment-phobic jerks.
   B. They're all tragically unlucky in love.
   C. All these women are die-hard commitment-phobes.

If you answered A, you'd only be partially right. If you answered B, you're way off, sistah! But if you answered C, then you would be 100 percent correct.

We all have that one girlfriend who's always in the midst of some personal crisis or emotional drama, the one who's always complaining how tragically unlucky in love she is, the one who's always stuck in destructive relationships with guys who won't make room in their medicine cabinet, introduce her to his parents, or even say "I love you."

Many of you have probably heard about the Peter Pan Syndrome, a common term used to describe men who refuse to grow up and make commitments. But what about the Tinker Bell Syndrome? There's been remarkably little written about Peter Pan's faithful companion. Yet the Tinker Bell character is an important one to explore, seeing how much in common she has with many of today's women. So who is Tinker Bell exactly, and what is this syndrome all about?

Much like the Disney character who spent her entire fairy-tale existence pining away for the elusive Peter Pan, real-life Tinker Bells are always getting involved with emotionally unavailable men who refuse to grow up, profess their undying love, and commit to them. In the classic tale of Peter Pan, Tinker Bell is hopelessly loyal to the unavailable hero, but in the end she never gets much attention from the adolescent object of her obsession. Tinker Bell is portrayed as a faithful fairy who follows Peter around everywhere, and while the relationship never goes beyond friendship, it's pretty clear that Tinker Bell is head over fairy heels for young Peter.

And that's what the Tinker Bell dilemma is all about: women who find themselves endlessly pining for and chasing an unavailable man in the hope that one day he will come to his senses and reciprocate their feelings. Whether he's already married to someone else, mentally unstable, or a player, there's always something terminally wrong with the men they date. And since all Tinker Bells swear that they would commit if only Peter Pan would come around, no one can really blame them for having commitment issues. After all, it's not their fault that they constantly find themselves trapped in dead-end relationships. Or is it?

Take Heather, for example. A successful boutique owner, she spent four years chasing after Greg, a handsome lawyer she met at a bar one night. She would scan his horoscope for clues, write long letters professing her undying love, and cry herself to sleep every night. Of course, Greg was terribly flattered. Not only was Heather attractive, but she was also (when she wasn't crying on the phone, of course) a dynamic person with an exciting personality. By some stroke of sheer luck, Greg finally realized, "Hmmm, maybe she *is* the one for me." Well, you can only imagine what happened next. After a brief moment of delirious triumph, Heather, like most Tinker Bells, went running for the door faster than you can say "skid marks."

In the end, it was about the fantasy of being with Greg, not actually the reality of the man himself, whom she later described as a self-obsessed, neurotic mama's boy who never once bothered to take her out to dinner. And while we can shake our head at poor Heather's predicament, I can't tell you how common this scenario is. Because when it comes to Tinker Bells, it's much easier, safer, and less threatening for them to pine away for a fantasy than to deal with the nitty-gritty reality of having a concrete relationship.

THE DOCTOR IS IN

One of the biggest signs of commitment-phobia is dating the wrong guy: being attracted to men who are emotionally unavailable, men who are forever bachelors, men who are married, men about town, men who don't want to be in relationships. It usually happens because the women are emotionally unavailable themselves.

—*Allison Moir-Smith, M.A.*

While some women prefer to think of themselves as victims in the game of love, in the end there really is no such thing. We're all ultimately responsible for our choices and the outcome of our romantic lives, whether we're conscious of what we're doing or not. Lest you blame your issues on your poor judgment about men, it's important to realize that commitment anxiety is the real culprit here and can drive perfectly sensible women into the arms of total derelicts. After all, dating men who are completely unavailable or inappropriate is a foolproof way to ensure that you, too, never have to make a commitment. And that is precisely why you Tinker Bells pick them in the first place. The question you have to answer is this. If you're choosing to be with someone who isn't ready for a serious relationship, what does that say about you? When in doubt, remember the golden rule: *IF YOU'RE WITH A COMMITMENT-PHOBE, YOU ARE A COMMITMENT-PHOBE!* After all, it does take one to know one.

THE CONFESSIONAL: Vicky, 28

I definitely have been choosing the wrong guys. I think I know that they are wrong from the start. There was this one guy, Manuel. I thought he was the most amazing man in the world. And he was definitely the best lover I ever had. I would go on and on about him, telling all my friends how into him I was. But I really didn't even know him. He was this thing that I just made up in my head. It didn't take me long to realize that. I guess it finally hit me when he fell in love with me and all I wanted to do was to get away from him. The same thing happened with Paul. I was really into him at first, thinking about him obsessively and worrying if he was going to call. I became really suspicious, and didn't even believe him when he told me he wasn't married. But as soon as I found out that he was available and liked me back, I was like, "Bye-bye."

? QUIZ: ARE YOU A TRUE TINKER BELL?

If you're always waiting for your commitment-phobic guy to come around, you may indeed be one yourself. So if you're ready to find out if you're a commitment-phobe hiding in Tinker Bell's clothing, take this quiz pronto!

Elina Furman

1. **You've been dating a man for three months and he suddenly leaves for a week without so much as a phone call. When he gets back, he tells you some crazy story about being abducted by aliens. What do you do?**
   A. Start doing research on the topic and offer to help him recuperate.
   B. Tell him you don't believe in aliens and demand an explanation, all the while planning your next date with him.
   C. Drop him without a second thought.

2. **How many of your boyfriends have your friends actually approved of?**
   A. They have pretty much hated all of them.
   B. They liked a few, but are always telling me I shouldn't settle for less than I deserve.
   C. Most of them, I think.

3. **Your mom calls you yet again, asking you when she can meet your latest boyfriend. You:**
   A. Tell her that his weekends are reserved for the wife and kids.
   B. Make up excuses—what with him always on the road, it's hard to set a definite time.
   C. Try your best to get back to her with a time and date.

4. **Your boss asks you to go out on an important business trip, which could be great for your career. But you and your guy have already made plans for a romantic weekend date. You:**
   A. Make up an excuse to tell your boss. Your guy has such a hard time committing to plans, you don't want to miss your chance.
   B. Call your guy and try to reschedule. If he agrees, then you'll go on the business trip.
   C. No-brainer! Go on the business trip. Your guy will understand.

5. **Your last fight was about:**
   A. The same thing we always fight about—I want a commitment and he doesn't.
   B. I saw him checking out another girl and he denied it.
   C. I don't remember . . . probably something stupid that he or I said.

6. **What's your idea of the perfect date?**
   A. Um . . . that he shows up.
   B. I don't know. Whatever he wants to do.
   C. A romantic dinner and good conversation.

7. **Breaking up is hard to do. How long did it take you to get over your last relationship?**
   A. We never really broke up. We still see each other on and off, which is basically whenever he calls me.
   B. I'm still getting over it. I keep hoping he'll change his mind.
   C. A few months. But I'm totally over him!

8. **When you arrive to meet your guy at a hot new restaurant, you notice him flirting with a busty version of Kate Moss. What do you do?**
   A. Freak out and tell the girl to keep her hands to herself.
   B. Confront him right there in the restaurant and accept his lame excuse.
   C. Go through with the date, but vow to seriously consider whether to keep dating him.

9. **When your guy tells you he's not ready for a serious relationship, how do you interpret it?**
   A. He's probably just stressed at work. Nothing that a night with me won't cure.
   B. He just needs more time. I have to work on being patient.
   C. That he's not interested in a serious relationship with me. Oh well, can't win 'em all.

10. **How often do you sit around hoping your love interest will call?**
    A. Pretty much all the time, since he rarely ever does.
    B. Sometimes, especially when he tells me he'll call and then forgets.
    C. He usually calls when he says he will, so not that often.

Scoring: To calculate your final score, assign a point value to each answer: 3 for every A, 2 for every B, and 1 for every C. Now add it all up to see how you rate.

23–30 Points: Totally Tinker Bell

Wow, you sure know how to pick 'em! Think about it: you're always with someone who's completely inept, and you're prone to making excuses just to keep on seeing him. So what exactly are you so afraid of? Does the prospect of a real relationship with someone who actually returns your feelings scare you that much? While you may think that you're all about finding a real commitment, your Tinker Bell ways say otherwise. That's right, actions speak louder than words. After all, there are plenty of guys who would be willing to return your feelings—not that you'd be interested in them if they ever did.

THE CONFESSIONAL: Karen, 32

I'm scared I'm going to meet a guy who wants to try to make a relationship work, and then I'll have to walk away. I always tend to go out with guys who are unattainable because they're not ready to settle down. It takes the pressure off me. The guy I'm with now has been married before and he's had many commitment issues, so I kind of thought of him as a safe person to date. But now things have changed, and he's gotten over his commitment issues and I'm dying to get out of the relationship.

15–22 Points: Just Tinkering

Look, no one's saying you have it easy. It's damn hard telling someone you want him in your life forever and ever, only to have him change his number, move to another country, or tell you he's gay. But time and time again, that might be precisely what's happening to you. While you definitely have all the traits of a Tinker Bell, give yourself points for being aware of your behavior. There's probably a small part of you that knows you're a sucker for loony Lotharios. You may even suspect that you're not ready for a serious relationship, or at least not right now. And though awareness is the first step to recovery, you'll have to do some serious work before you're ready to renounce your Tinker Bell title for good.

14 or Fewer Points: Peter? Who's Peter?

A Tinker Bell? Not you! You wouldn't dream of wasting your time on someone who's not into you. And while you may have occasionally dated someone because you thought he was a challenge, one-sided relationships are simply not your cup of java. While the Peter Pans of the world go running wild, you're not about to sit on the sidelines waiting for them to come around. After all, if you wanted to live in a fairy tale, you'd read one to yourself before going to sleep every night.

TINKER BELL PROTESTS: "I'M NOT A TINKER BELL, I'M JUST . . ."

If you're a Tinker Bell, you probably have a whole slew of carefully worked-out rebuttals. After all, you're one of the most complicated types of commitment-phobes. Just try convincing a Tinker Bell that she has commitment issues—even Mother Teresa would find herself getting impatient. Think about it. You're always going on about how much in love you are, how ready you are for a commitment, how life would be perfect if he just returned your feelings. You simply have no idea that dating relationship duds is a sure sign that you're not ready for anything serious, either. Just to be on the safe side, join your fellow Tinks in saying, "I'm not a Tinker Bell, I'm just . . ."

1. **"I'm Just Unlucky in Love."** Sound familiar? I really can't understand why so many women cling to the notion that they are somehow victims in the game of love. Let's get one thing straight: there's simply no such thing as being "unlucky in love." As with everything in life, we create our own luck by making good decisions, working hard, and spotting trouble before it spots us. So when in doubt, remember the golden rule: *you're not unlucky in love, you're just good at being single!*

    And since we're on the subject of luck, a card analogy seems only appropriate. While we can't control what cards we're dealt, we can decide which hand we're going to play. You wouldn't want to play a losing hand unless you planned to lose. The same thing goes for the men in your life. Those of you who don't want a long-term relationship will often bet on men who won't offer one. But get one thing straight: *you* choose the hands you play and the men you date, and these choices say a lot more about you than all your magazine subscriptions to *The Knot* and *Modern Bride* combined. Changing your luck with men is as easy as making better choices. So whether or not you think you're commitment-phobic, understand that admitting your ambivalence and taking responsibility for your romantic choices can be very empowering. And while it might hurt a bit to admit, "I was wrong," it's better than always yelling, "I was wronged!"

THE DOCTOR IS IN

If you're always getting involved with unavailable men and you don't see that necessarily as a problem, it could be that you do not want to get involved in a relationship but are too afraid to admit it to yourself because you feel bad for even having that thought.

—*Dr. Michael S. Broder*

2. **"I'm Just into the Challenge."** When it comes to love, Tinker Bells are often in it for the thrill of the chase rather than the actual person. You tend to want what you cannot have, because if you actually got the guy to commit, it wouldn't be long until you lost interest. The more likely scenario is that you won't rest until you've converted him from a commitment-phobe to a devoted dude—only to drop him a week later when he starts calling too much. You're the reason they invented the saying "Nice guys finish last." There's nothing less appealing to you than a guy who's up-front, lays his cards on the table, and tells you how he really feels about you. No, that would be too easy.

For many Tinker Bells, the perfect guy is someone who is either involved with someone else, married, or suffering from his own commitment issues. So is it any surprise that you constantly find yourself chasing after guys who are unavailable or even trying to change guys who have told you point-blank that they're not interested? Those of you who find yourself more attracted to a man who's already taken than to someone who's available are definitely not ready for a serious commitment. If you want a challenge, admit it to yourself and have fun pursuing the object of your temporary affections (I personally prefer a good game of Scrabble). But don't kid yourself for one second that you're interested in having a committed relationship, because it's hardly the same thing.

THE CONFESSIONAL: Daphne, 44

My love of the "thrill of the hunt" and new challenges has caused me to feel very constrained in a relationship. I tend to get bored easily once I know a guy is into me, and act like a maniac so he will break up with me and then I won't have to feel the guilt of initiating the breakup. Guys with other girlfriends are always a favorite because they don't make demands and aren't very needy.

3. **"I'm Just a Hopeless Romantic."** Oh, that's so sweet. Pining away for an elusive guy *can* be so romantic. There's listening to sad love songs, drunk-dialing him every night, and hooking up with random strangers who bear even the slightest resemblance to him. What could possibly be more romantic than that? While it can be reassuring to think of yourself as an amorous idealist, waiting around for that thickheaded knight to sweep you off your feet is not really the best way to banish those Tinker Bell blues.

Not that it's entirely your fault, of course. Women have been susceptible to fantasies and fairy tales for ages. Problem is, most of these stories are completely unrealistic. I mean, unlike Rapunzel, we all know that hair only grows two inches every three months. And Tinker Bell's very existence depends on fantasy, since it's our collective belief in fairies that keeps her alive.

10 SIGNS YOU'RE DATING A COMMITMENT-PHOBE

If your guy exhibits any of the traits below, you can be sure he's more than a little commitment-shy. But don't start climbing on your high horse just yet. Every time you check off a statement, remind yourself that it's your own anxiety that led you to date this guy in the first place. If you haven't figured it out yet, the mathematical equation for commitment-phobia is simple: his level of commitment anxiety is directly proportional to your own.

	CHECK OFF
1. He only wants to see you one night of the week or on weekends.	
2. He won't call you his girlfriend after three to six months of dating.	
3. He doesn't invite you to meet his friends or parents after six months of dating.	
4. He keeps you off balance by breaking dates and popping in unannounced.	
5. He blows hot and cold in the relationship. One day he can't live without you, the next day he needs his space.	
6. He never talks about the future with you.	
7. He only gives you his cell phone number.	
8. He doesn't share any of his experiences with family or past relationships.	
9. He won't tell you he loves you, even after you say it to him.	
10. He insists on seeing other women.	

So why do you persist in believing in your fantasies despite all the evidence showing that he's not the right one for you? Because it keeps you from the other, far scarier reality of inviting real commitment into your life. So if your friends and family are always calling you a romantic, don't flatter yourself.

It's not necessarily a compliment. After all, being a romantic is about doing caring things for the person you love and who loves you back—not some imaginary boyfriend with a wife and two kids.

TOP TINKER BELL HANG-UPS

You Tinker Bells have it rough. What with all those nights spent waiting for your guy to call, it's no wonder you feel so down on love. But did you ever stop to think that maybe you're hooked on the drama, that maybe you're more into the highs and lows that these guys provide than a stable relationship? Check out this list to find out if you've ever fallen prey to these common Tinker Bell hang-ups.

1. What's *He* Thinking?

Open any women's magazine or relationship book and you'll find plenty of sound advice about understanding your man. There are the top 10 signs he thinks you're fat, what he really means when he says he's going to the grocery store, and other tricks of the trade for decoding his secret "caveman" language. For some reason, the media get off on making you study your man like a lab rat in a cage. Then they usually fill your head with tips on how to use that knowledge to "get" him to commit to you.

I really believe that all of us would be much better off if women would just stop trying so hard to figure men out. If you're constantly worrying about what your man wants, thinks, and is doing, how much time does that leave for you? That's right. The one thing these tomes of wisdom don't talk about is *you*. There are no quizzes for finding out if *you're* really into him, no advice on how to tell if *you're* ready for a commitment, or anything even remotely helpful about finding out who *you* are.

The problem with being a Tinker Bell is that you tend to spend most of your time thinking about the object of your obsession rather than thinking about yourself. It's easier to channel all that mental energy outward rather than turning the focus inward. After all, you might discover some painful truths, such as why

Elina Furman

you're scared of being in a real relationship or what is really driving you to be with someone who doesn't return your feelings. So while you may be fascinated by the workings of the male mind, you can't possibly begin to understand anyone until you figure out what's behind your own behavior.

2. Nothing Good Ever Comes Easy

Having been weaned on the Puritan work ethic, some of us have internalized the idea that whatever comes easy has no value, that rewards earned through hard work are that much sweeter. We assume that men who fall easily for us are not worth having, and guys who are ambivalent are somehow the bigger, better prize. Popular clichés that say "Nothing worthwhile is easy," "If it isn't hurting, it isn't working," and "No pain, no gain" have programmed us to believe that pain and hardship are necessary by-products of looking for love. Well, that's a whole lot of bunk! While this philosophy may help you get your lazy butt into the gym or office, it's completely useless when it comes to your dating life. In fact, it can mess you up big time.

If you're using the harder-they-come measure to gauge whether a guy is good enough to hang with, you're going to be very disappointed in the long run. Just because someone is interested in you and legitimately wants to get to know you doesn't mean that that person is somehow less swoon-worthy than the guy who gives you the runaround and won't return your phone calls. While that reasoning may have made sense to our hard-working, nose-to-the-grindstone ancestors, I'm sure they didn't mean for you to trade an attractive, good-hearted guy for someone who's got a criminal record, lives with his parents, and picks his nose in public. So remember: while he may be harder to get, it doesn't necessarily mean he's worth any of the effort.

3. The Perils of Dating Up

Warning: what I'm about to say may be construed as offensive, politically incorrect, and downright rude. Whether you're an attractive MBA, a dowdy librarian, or a cultured fashionista, it's important that you date on your own level. Before you go ballistic, stop and think about what I'm saying. I can't stress enough how important it is to have a realistic idea about who you are and what kind of men will be attracted to you. Okay, we all have one overweight guy friend who only wants to date supermodels (think *Shallow Hal*, the movie), claiming that every normal woman he meets isn't good-looking enough. And while we can laugh at his delusional dating agenda, it's important for us to consider if we're victims of the same mind-set.

While some women just happen to have very high standards, there's no use always going for the hottest, richest, and most successful guy in the room. It's a simple case of supply and demand. Most women want the six-foot-tall, attractive CEO. But since the demand is so high, there's usually not enough of them to go around. And besides, not only do these fine specimens of manhood have a million girls vying for their attention, they also have major egos to boot.

So while it's normal to be attracted to these types, it's also important to have a realistic idea about your chances of actually having a relationship with them. After all, just because I've considered building a shrine to Owen Wilson's greatness, that doesn't mean I'm going to put my love life on hold until he comes around (Owen, if you're out there . . .). Admiring someone from afar is all well and good. But remember, if you're too busy pining away for someone unattainable, you may lose out on the chance to date perfectly fine men who are more up your alley.

THE CONFESSIONAL: Thya, 25

One night, I met this guy at a roof party. He was really hot and was hysterically funny. He was also pretty confident and seemed to know everyone. When I asked my friends who he was and whether he had a girlfriend, they kind of rolled their eyes at me and told me he probably had more than one. But I didn't care. I got his number that night and called him the next day. He seemed kind of weird on the phone, asking where he met me, and finally agreed to get coffee, even though I'm sure he had no idea who I was. The date was horrible. He was distracted the whole time and left after an hour. I should have known he wasn't interested, but I pursued him anyway and tried to be friends. After a while, he had me picking up his laundry and cleaning his apartment, but I didn't care. I thought he was just making up excuses to be with me. One night, I saw him out with another girl and I lost it. But it wasn't really his fault. He had told me a couple of times that he wasn't attracted to me; I just didn't want to hear it. I'm seeing someone great right now, and even though he's not drop-dead gorgeous or the funniest person I know, he's all those things to me.

GET OVER IT: SUREFIRE STRATEGIES

Let's get one thing straight. I'm not here to make you change your ways. If you're happy being in an on-and-off relationship and wondering when or if he's ever going to call again, skip this section entirely. But if you're tired of dead-end relationships with emotional nitwits and want to graduate from Tinker Bell to Wendy sometime before the next millennium, check out these answers to your most pressing questions.

Q. *"If you're saying that two people should always be on the same page in a relationship, I disagree. I always think someone is more committed and you have to wait for the other person to catch up."*

A. You make a great point. Relationships are a complicated lot. Rarely are they ever completely fifty-fifty. It's not at all uncommon for someone to be more head over heels in love than the other person, and even to have that dynamic shift several times throughout the course of a relationship. Take this couple I know, Greg and Dana. He chased her for months—calling her, taking her out to expensive dinners, the works. Dana, on the other hand, wasn't buying any of it. He was more serious than some of the guys she was dating, and he wasn't her physical ideal. So she continued to see other people for the first six months, telling Greg that she didn't want to commit prematurely. Eventually, after getting to know him, Dana became more comfortable with the prospect of being with him. She would find herself thinking about Greg and slowly phased out her other boyfriends so they could spend more time together. And that's when she dropped the L-bomb and told him she was in love.

Naturally, she expected him to become overwhelmed with happiness and run around the apartment screaming, "Hallelujah." But instead of being happy, he was completely taken aback. He had been waiting for those words for so long that once it finally happened, he was completely weirded out. After a long conversation with plenty of re-criminations on both sides, he told her he needed some space. Fortunately, the story had a happy ending. After two weeks without her, Greg came back and professed his stupidity, and they've been dating ever since.

The moral of the story? Relationships are like dancing. It's one step back and two steps forward. So how do you know if you're a Tinker Bell or if you're just on the wrong side of the relationship two-step? Well, it depends on your past relationship patterns. If you're always finding yourself getting involved in one-sided arrangements, that might just be the tip-off you need to admit that you purposely seek out these types of guys to avoid having a relationship. But if it only happens once in a while, you're probably not a full-blown Tinker Bell—in which case you might want to give your guy some time before hatching a silent ultimatum.

THE CONFESSIONAL: Sophie, 39

For years I dated all these guys and it would always be the same story. We'd date for a couple of months and then I would try getting closer, at which point they always pulled back. I thought all relationships were

like that until I met Dan. With the other guys, I was always scared to reveal my feelings, thinking they were going to judge me. But Dan made it so easy. After a few weeks of dating, we started talking about our goals and hopes for the future. I had never met a guy who was so open to talking about family and kids. It was really amazing. We were always on the same wavelength. It took meeting him to make me realize how one-sided and immature all those other relationships were.

Q. "I don't get it. So are you saying I should dump my boyfriend because he won't commit to me?"

A. Absolutely not. I would never tell you that "he's just not that into you, so dump him!" After all, it's not your boyfriend's fault that you picked him out of a sea of commitment-ready guys just so you could avoid dealing with your own intimacy issues. No, I would never advise you to take such drastic measures until you take a good hard look at the one person responsible for your predicament: *you!*

Okay, so how do you do that? If you haven't done so already, please take the commitment-phobia quiz in the beginning of this book. If you found out that you truly have some misgivings about sustaining a committed relationship, it's time you asked yourself some tough questions about your situation.

1. If my boyfriend told me there was zero chance that he would commit to me, I would still want to stay with him.

TRUE   FALSE

2. I enjoy the ups and down of our relationship. I like that he keeps me on edge.   TRUE   FALSE

3. I feel that the good outweighs the bad in our relationship.

TRUE   FALSE

4. He makes me feel happy, loved, and secure, despite not wanting to commit to me.   TRUE   FALSE

5. I'm happy with him at least 80 percent of the time.

TRUE   FALSE

ANATOMY OF A BREAKUP WITH A COMMITMENT-PHOBE

- You tell him you want to break up over dinner.
- He takes it graciously, telling you that you'll always have a special place in his heart even though he doesn't want a commitment.
- A week or two passes. You cry, drag yourself late into work every day, and either gain or lose weight.
- As soon as you feel that you are regaining your balance, he will call to ask you how you've been holding up. After all, breaking up doesn't mean you can't still be friends.
- Another week will go by, at which point he will e-mail you to set up a friendly date. What are a few drinks between two old friends?
- You think he's calling you because he really wants to get back together with you, and so you agree to go out with him just to see what he has to say.
- When you meet, he tells you he misses you and wants things to go back to the way they were.
- You ask him if he is willing to commit. He says he's still not ready.
- You decide never to see him again, and have to start the getting-over-him process all over again.

Pencils down. If you answered false four or more times, you're definitely doing yourself a major disservice by sticking with this guy. That's not to say that some women aren't content and even happy to be with a noncommittal boyfriend. You, however, don't seem to fall into that category. And while your relationship anxiety might have led you to pursue this guy, your new commitment-friendly attitude should help you leave him for good.

Q. *"Okay, you're right. I'm so done with commitment-phobic guys, but my ex keeps coming back even though he says he still doesn't want a commitment. What do I do?"*

A. Good for you! Now that he's history, you can begin to look at some of the reasons you attracted a Peter Pan in the first place. But before you do that, you'll need to clear the decks and make sure he gets the message loud and clear. Unfortunately, breaking up with this type of guy is a sure way to get him to start chasing you all over again, because as we all know, commitment-phobic guys have trouble committing to anything—either starting a relationship or ending one. Once the fear of getting too close is gone, he'll remember all the reasons he liked you in the first place, such as your beautiful smile, your cute bunny pajamas, and your famous poppy-seed muffins. But as much as he may miss you, remember that his trying to get back together in no way indicates that things will be different the second time around. So cut the cord and don't look back.

Q. *"So how do I avoid getting involved with commitment-phobic men in the first place? It's not like these guys come with warning labels."*

A. It never fails. There are some women who seem to draw commitment-phobes to them like flies. It's almost as if they're wearing Eau de Commitment-Phobe perfume. The reason Tinker Bells are so attractive to Peter Pans is because they sense you're not ready for anything serious, and pursuing you seems like a safer bet. Time and time again, these guys make a beeline for Tinker Bells, despite the fact that the women have done nothing overt to attract them. Or have they? In the end, there are a million and one signals that give these guys a green light. It could be pheromones, the way you tilt your head, the way you sip your drink. And while I can give you plenty of advice about how to stop attracting these hit-and-run guys, the best way to avoid these duds is to work through your own Tinker Bell issues once and for all.

TINKER BELL RECAP

How quickly we forget. It seems like it was just six pages ago that we went over all this. Here's a quick recap.

- Remember the golden rule: if you're with a commitment-phobe, you *are* a commitment-phobe.

- Dating men who are completely unavailable or inappropriate is a foolproof way to ensure that you, too, never have to make a commitment.

- You're not unlucky in love, you're just good at staying single.

- If a guy who's already taken is more appealing to you than someone who's available, you need some serious commitment coaching.

- The mathematical equation for commitment phobia is simple: his level of commitment anxiety is directly proportional to your own.

- Don't date up. If you're only dating guys whom you think are a major catch, good luck ever catching them.

- Playing hard to get with a commitment-phobic man is like waving a stick of dynamite in front of a pyromaniac.

- Don't act like a sheep in wolf's clothing. If you're finally ready for a commitment, make sure your words and actions match up.

6

The Free Spirit

HOBBIES: Drums, origami, naked Twister, knitting

READS: *Jane, Blender, BUST,* Anaïs Nin

LIKES: Motorcycles, talking dirty in French, breaking the ice

HATES: Suits, grammar Nazis, guilt, conformity

MUSIC: Massive Attack, Air, PJ Harvey, Nina Simone

ONLINE: Personal blog, SuicideGirls.com, Nerve.com

IN HER ROOM: Original artwork/photography, candles, sewing machine, fishnets, old guitar

THE FIVE ITEMS SHE CAN'T LIVE WITHOUT:

1. Passport
2. Spicy food
3. Flip-flops
4. Thrift stores
5. Perpetual motion

*I*f you've ever met this changeling woman, you'd know that this is only a portrait, not a stereotype. After all, you'd be hard pressed to find anything stereotypical about our fourth type of commitment-phobe. So who is the Free Spirit exactly? Well, for starters she's a little bit quirky, totally wild, and always unpredictable. Whether teetering on three-inch heels through the streets of Paris or stomping barefoot through the park, she's a bundle of frenetic energy and contradictions, an incorrigible force of nature that you can't help stopping to watch.

While you wouldn't want to label her, even Free Spirits have some traits in common. Most of them get bored quickly and need a lot of friends, activities, and diversions to satisfy their wanderlust. While they're usually creative by nature, the Free Spirit doesn't have to be an artist to qualify. Whether it's through activism, travel, partying, entrepreneurialism, or all of the above, the Free Spirit is someone who thrives on change and lives by instinct. After all, it's not about how she earns her living, but rather about how she lives her life—brazenly, shamelessly, and always unconventionally.

Where can you find her? Well, good luck ever trying to. She's here, there, and everywhere all at once. Whether she's painting up a storm, going on a road trip, or flitting from one party to the next, the Free Spirit is always on the move. Not surprisingly, this commitment-phobic archetype has difficulty laying down roots and finds it nearly impossible to commit to any one relationship. She prefers the initial stages of the relationship, characterized by passion and extreme feelings, and panics when the alliance settles into a comfortable routine. Her idea of the perfect union? Two people wake up, have hot passionate sex, stare dreamily into each other's eyes, and then go out to a late lunch to discuss their latest masterpieces or philosophy. Miraculously, they also somehow find the time to pay the bills, keep the studio apartment clean, and walk Kubrick, the family dog. This is one girl who wants to do everything in a big way, especially when it comes to matters of the heart.

While the Free Spirit may be a ripe subject for films and novels, the real-world version is far more problematic. Despite their haphazard and rebellious attitudes toward love, Free Spirits crave permanency as much as they fear it. They are deeply scared of commitment and tend to use wanderlust and independence as an excuse to ward off possible entanglements. And there's the rub: *as much as the Free Spirit fears routine, boredom, and giving up her freedom, she also longs for a stable, loving companion who will support her life goals and passions.*

It's no surprise, then, that many of you are worried that any relationship, however good, will undermine your personal development, life goals, and creativity. In this chapter, you'll find out how your attempts to protect your creative outlets and freedom can actually backfire, leaving you with less time, energy, and inspiration to develop and grow. It will also show you how to approach relationships with the same excitement and sense of adventure that you reserve for your daily life, so you can create a healthy balance of personal space, freedom, and companionship.

THE CONFESSIONAL: Ivy, 37

I paint and read and enjoy walks by myself in the local parks. I have academic, creative, and career goals, and none of them requires a partner. I wouldn't want to pursue a relationship simply to have one and not be able to devote the time and attention necessary to maintain it. My freedom is valuable in that I can see whomever I want to see when I want to see them, spend my money as I like, and cook/eat on my own schedule. It would be selfish of me to marry, given my disposition. I use up a lot of energy to commit to work/school/learning, etc., and when I get home all I want to do is wind down, relax, and not talk to anyone. Sometimes I feel that worrying about another person and their needs could be very draining. I feel a sense of obligation to perform at work and in my other activities. Sometimes I also feel pressure to "perform" in relationships, and although I recognize this could be self-imposed, it's still a burden. It's a matter of time, and if you spend the majority of your time devoting attention and interest to another person, you lose time to spend on your creative pursuits or whatever. A relationship wouldn't rob me of my freedom, identity, or creative spirit, but it might involve compromising all of the above.

FREE SPIRIT TYPECASTING

It's almost impossible to reduce the Free Spirit down to just one type. In fact, this quirky commitment-phobe comes in a variety of shapes, personalities, and attitudes. Here's your chance to find out which of the Free Spirit profiles you fit most.

1. **The Party Girl.** Sassy, savvy, and clued in to all the hottest events, the Party Girl lives for the nightlife, happening outings, and any type

of social diversion. A little bit hedonistic, she can't stand to be alone, be bored, or stay at any one party for too long.

2. **The Humanitarian.** This woman won't rest until she's saved every orphan, cured world hunger, and established world peace. When it comes to relationships, the Humanitarian needs someone as socially conscious as she is, or at least someone who will support her efforts.

3. **The Artist.** With her exacting standards and strong visionary powers, it's not surprising to find the Artist holed up in some studio or writing into the wee hours of the night. Whether it's floral arrangement, painting, or playing the piano, the Artist has a strong need to express herself in everything she does.

4. **The Vagabond.** "Have lipstick will travel" is the Vagabond's motto. Seeing the world, traveling to exotic ports of call, and mingling with locals, the Vagabond will always go back to her first love, which is the open road and the prospect of unlimited possibilities.

 QUIZ: ARE YOU A FREE SPIRIT?

We all have a little bit of the Free Spirit within us. You know, those days when you wear the studded belt or go to a protest rally. But no matter how artsy or bohemian you are, there are some women who just can't be pinned down (not for long, anyway). So whether you think you're a total maverick or just a bit fancy-free, take this quiz to find out how free-spirited you really are.

1. When getting dressed for a party, you usually choose:
   A. Something offbeat and unusual that I'm sure no one else will be wearing.
   B. Something comfortable with a few quirky accessories to spice it up.
   C. A trendy new look that I saw in a magazine.

2. **Your idea of the perfect vacation goes something like this:**

   A. An exotic trip to Costa Rica, Brazil, or Southeast Asia with no itinerary.
   B. A yoga spa retreat.
   C. A cruise ship getaway with all-inclusive meals and drinks so I can relax.

3. **Your inspirations lean toward these people:**

   A. Joan of Arc, the Dalai Lama, Henry Thoreau.
   B. Oprah Winfrey, Charlotte Brontë, Angelina Jolie.
   C. Martha Stewart, Marge Simpson, Kelly Ripa.

4. **Your date calls you to make plans for tonight, but you're not sure you want to go. Which of these date itineraries would make you change your mind?**

   A. A trip to the tattoo parlor and then a secret rock concert at an underground bar.
   B. Salsa dancing followed by Ethiopian food.
   C. Dinner at the most exclusive restaurant in town.

5. **Most of the guys you date can be described as:**

   A. Weird, eccentric, and borderline crazy.
   B. Spontaneous and fun.
   C. Solid and dependable.

6. **Your friend invites you to her belly dancing class, but you've never tried it. You:**

   A. Are so in! You even unearth an old skirt and a belly-baring top that are perfect for the class.
   B. Think about it for a few hours and then agree to go.
   C. Say no. You're a terrible dancer. And besides, what possible use would you have for belly dancing skills?

7. **Who is your favorite romantic couple of all time?**

   A. Heathcliff and Catherine
   B. Mark Antony and Cleopatra
   C. Robin Hood and Maid Marian

8. **How would you describe your sex life?**

   A. Anything goes and usually does. I'm very experimental.
   B. Somewhat creative, I guess.
   C. Pretty standard, but it suits me fine.

9. **If you suddenly had a financial windfall, what would be your first purchase?**
   A. Some original artwork and a trip around the world.
   B. A house by the water, where I could laze around and just do my thing.
   C. Shopping spree! I could finally buy all the designer bags and clothes I've been eyeing.

10. **When was the last time you worked in an office?**
   A. I would rather die than sit in a cubicle all day!
   B. I work or temp at an office on an as-needed basis, depending on how much I need the money.
   C. Always have. I prefer a structured environment to working at home.

Scoring: To calculate your final score, assign a point value to each answer: 3 for every A, 2 for every B, and 1 for every C. Now add it all up to get your score.

23–30 Points: Boho Princess

Aren't you a rebel? You're anything but conventional and would rather die than date someone who owns more than one tie. Much like the hippies of the past, you're all about experimenting, pushing boundaries, and following your inner muse. Your taste in men tends to run toward bad-boy rebels or artsy visionaries. While it's totally groovy that you're spontaneous and live for the moment, you may want to stop and smell the karma. It's one thing to live life as it comes, but try not to get too careless when it comes to matters of the heart.

THE CONFESSIONAL: Nicole, 24

I guess it's just because I like change and I hate routine. A marriage is like any other commitment in that you are required to do certain things and forbidden to do others. It is restricting, whether it is a happy marriage or not. It's kind of like a job—you can't just do anything you want. You have to work from nine to five and do certain things that are

> required of you while you are there. You may love your job, but there are restrictions. I currently work as a bartender, so I'm not sure where I will be next year. I have no rules. I am the boss of me and any choice I make affects only me. I never make plans. I am famous for saying maybe to everything. People usually hate it, but I don't think I will ever change that. There are also a lot of times that I just don't show up somewhere or even answer the phone.

15–22 Points: Free to Be Me

Independent and artistic, you crave lots of time alone to develop your talents. And why shouldn't you? Like Ellen DeGeneres, your life's probably about dancing to your own tune. After all, you probably want to contribute something unique to the world, and you admire feisty women who have defied the odds. With all the emphasis you put on your work and talents, it's not surprising that there have been times in your life when you were torn between your dedication to your work and your desire for relationships. Just make sure your need for freedom and creativity doesn't stand in the way of making commitments that could potentially enrich your life and your art.

14 or Fewer Points: In the Box

Less Joan Baez and more Joan Collins, you think nothing of following the less-traveled path, so long as it's paved, smooth, and has all the road signs clearly marked. Who cares if you're not into breaking the rules, opening your chakras, or finding the goddess within? Not all of us can stand the uncertainty of living life on the edge. While you may want to try walking on the wild side every now and then, your steady and sober approach to relationships should also be commended.

TOP FREE SPIRIT PROTESTS:
"I'M NOT A FREE SPIRIT, I JUST . . ."

So when did "free spirit" become such a dirty word? It hasn't. There's absolutely nothing wrong with wanting to run with the wolves, tap into your creativity, and chase your dreams. It's only problematic when you start using your free-spiritedness as an excuse to ward off potential commitment and avoid dealing with your intimacy issues. While following your bliss and being creative may be noble causes, so is your love life. That brings us back to the same place. Repeat after me: "I'm not a Free Spirit, I just . . ."

1. **"I Just Haven't Met Someone Who Shares My Passions."**
No doubt your passions are important to you. Whether you're a dedicated activist, painter, traveler, or musician, you've probably made your interests a central part of your life. But does that mean that your partner has to share every single one of them? Not necessarily.

The idea that one person can fulfill you completely is unrealistic, especially since as a Free Spirit, you probably have a zillion and one different preoccupations at any given time. Just think about all your amazing friends. If someone told you that you'd have to pick just one, that would be kind of freaky. All of a sudden, no matter how much you love your best friend, you'd come up with dozens of things that are wrong with her/him. Or what if someone told you to pick one interest or hobby? That would be kind of hard, too, considering how each one enriches you in a completely different way. So why in the world would you ask that of your significant other?

The all-or-nothing mentality can put a lot of pressure on your love interests. Just because your boyfriend hates independent films doesn't mean you can't go see one alone or with a friend. And what's the big deal if he doesn't know a Dadaist from a Surrealist or a haiku from a limerick? That doesn't mean you have to give him the heave-ho. After all, no one person can fulfill all your needs or "complete" you. That's why you have friends for lively conversation, your man for caring and support, your colleagues for professional feedback, and your outside interests that keep you feeling vital and creative. The bottom line: as long as he's not stopping you from doing what you want and supports your passions, there's no reason to let a good thing go.

THE CONFESSIONAL: Celia, 41

I like to do things, meet people, and have fun, and most of my boyfriends want to stay in. If I'm not happy in a relationship, I regularly bring up future plans that don't involve them, such as traveling extensively for long periods of time and even moving. I always make it seem like I am only around temporarily, until I move on to bigger and better things. It's amazing that I ever have boyfriends, isn't it? For me to be happy in a relationship, I have to feel like we have an intellectual connection. He has to be intelligent, spiritual, and willing to live spontaneously and join me in my adventures. He has to understand and appreciate all my strange ideas and opinions and creative spirit. The perfect man would support my dreams/plans/ideals and want to live the same way as me. He would want me to do everything that I needed to do in life. He wouldn't hold me back, even if it meant me running off for six months in Europe to travel alone and write a book. He would think it was great and he would have his own fabulous life going on at home and he would be there when I returned and I would be okay with him doing the same thing. But I don't think it will ever happen, because a man like that doesn't exist, does he?

2. **"I Just Think Relationships And Creativity Are Incompatible."** The notion that great art requires pain and suffering may be a cliché, but it's a pervasive one. There's the idea floating around that creativity demands that you be depressed, on edge, and constantly restless. Whenever we think of an artist, we imagine a broody type—wearing all black, smoking cigarettes, and downing their fourth espresso of the morning in a dingy coffee shop. And while it's true that many artists, such as Virginia Woolf, Vincent van Gogh, and even Elizabeth Wurtzel, were extremely creative during their most turbulent years, they accomplished all this *despite* their internal turmoil, not *because* of it.

Sharing this common belief, many of you Free Spirits worry that once you get into a happy, comfortable relationship you won't be motivated to create or pursue your life goals—

that you'll be so happy and content lying in the arms of your beloved that the idea of getting up and doing some hard creative work or traveling around the world will seem unappealing. And while some of your goals may fade into the background in the beginning stages of any relationship, most of you will find that you can happily resume your work once the fervor of the initial passion has subsided. In fact, once you're free of the chaos and emotional drama of unstable, go-nowhere relationships, you may even discover that being in a committed relationship actually gives you more motivation to pursue your passions in the future.

THE DOCTOR IS IN

A woman can be married to her muse. It doesn't necessarily have to be creative—it could be a career or something else, too. Basically for her to enter into a committed relationship, it has to be a three-way relationship: the woman, her art, and the man. She wants a man who can relate not only to her, but also to her art. And the fear is that he only wants to be with her and doesn't love, support, and adore her art as much as he loves, supports, and adores her. So the belief that some women may hold is that it's not possible to love and support both, and that can lead her to choose her creativity or her career over the man. It's a belief she has, but it's not necessarily true. If she would open up to the possibility that a man could support both, then that could be possible. But the blinders are on, and she can't see that it's an option. And in fact, there are men who have traditional expectations about sex roles and who don't want a third party, in this case the art, in the relationship. But that's not true of all men. It's less and less true as we get away from our rigid expectations of gender identities and about roles in relationships.

—*Dr. Deborah Anapol*

3. **"I Just Need a Lot of Time Alone."** Free Spirits tend to be an introspective and complicated lot. Even when you look like

Elina Furman

you're just staring into space, you may be composing your next song or planning your next adventure. As a result, the idea of sharing your physical and mental space with someone can be extremely unnerving. It's no wonder you're so guarded about committing yourself and your time. You're probably used to having a "room of your own" and are scared to have your space and time infringed upon.

But you don't have to sacrifice a relationship for the sake of your life calling. You just have to choose your partners more carefully. Who's to say you can't find your own love patron, or at least someone considerate enough to close the door behind him when he sees you working? While it's true that some partners will be threatened by your devotion to your goals and try to curtail your activity, many others are inspired by a passionate woman and would gladly give you all the space you need. So if you need to take a month off to go to a workshop or want to spend a week partying in Croatia, you should expect no less than complete and total support—and, of course, return the favor should your partner need to do some exploring on his own. In the end, dating people who make excessive demands on your time is a sure way to develop commitment anxiety since it will only reconfirm your fears that you can't have it all.

TOP FREE SPIRIT HANG-UPS

It never ceases to amaze me. Free Spirits go on and on about how they have no hang-ups, how they go with the flow, how cool they are with everything. But when it comes to looking at all the ways they avoid relationships, Free Spirits are out the door in no time flat, ready to set sail on yet another adventure or a Peace Corps mission just to avoid dealing with their fear of permanence.

The most important thing to remember is that a true Free Spirit is someone who is unafraid. After all, it takes a lot of courage to be intimate and commit to one person. So if you're

MR. NEEDY VERSUS MR. SECURE

Let's face it—it's not every man who can handle an offbeat and independent woman like you. The partner you choose will have to be confident, relaxed, and secure in your relationship. How else could he possibly hope to keep up with you? Here's how to separate the secure men from the needy boys.

MR. NEEDY

1. Likes to spend hours talking on the phone

2. Says "I love you" on the third date

3. Asks you for detailed accounts of your day and plans

4. Wants to know how you're "feeling" all the time

5. Complains that you don't spend enough time together

6. Is critical of your friends and outside interests

7. Doesn't leave your side at a party

8. Only wants to hang out with you

9. Freaks out when you go on vacation without him

MR. SECURE

1. Calls you once a day to make plans

2. Takes his time saying the L-word

3. Doesn't question you about your plans, unless you volunteer the information

4. Is sensitive to your feelings without always having to quiz you

5. Enjoys spending time with your friends and trying new things with you

6. Is proud and supports your talents and personal goals

7. Circulates at parties and is open to meeting new people

8. Has a wide circle of friends and many interests

9. Asks you to bring back something unique from your vacations

too busy pursuing your creative goals and never stop to experience true intimacy, you're not living up to the label, no matter how many Nobel prizes you win or paintings you sell. Still not convinced? Check out these common Free Spirit mistakes.

1. Only Date Other Free Spirits

For someone so open-minded, you can be very rigid about the men you date. Let's take a look at who exactly that is.

- Bad boys who make you feel alive and slightly dangerous
- Brooding hipster types who are constantly broke
- Wannabe rock stars who drink too much
- Wanderers who are never in one place too long
- Younger men who never pose any serious risk of commitment

While all these men may appeal to your vagabond spirit, they may actually be standing in the way of your self-development. After all, it's not easy dating this motley crew. There are the constant breakdowns, missed dates, never-ending tirades against the "system," and all sorts of other issues. What with all their antics and dramas, it's a wonder you have any time to focus on yourself.

The paradox of dating these types is that while they can be very stimulating and even inspiring, it can be very draining to have two high-maintenance people in the same relationship, leaving you with little time to develop your innate gifts and focus on your own career passions. So while I'm not saying these types of men are the devil's spawn, they can be more challenging than your average Joe and leave you with even less time to focus on your work.

And while we're on the subject, what's so wrong or even average about Joe? You know, the bankers, financiers, and Alex P. Keatons of the world. While it may be amusing to typecast them and ridicule their PDAs and constant stock quote checking, that would be too simple for someone as complicated as you. In fact, stereotyping men on the basis of what they do is not at all free-spirited (it's more shallow-spirited) and can prevent you from meeting like-minded people. Of course, there's no rule you have to give non-artsy types a chance, but by dating different types of guys who don't fit the "alternative" mold, you may find that you're able to put even more energy and effort into your personal goals when you don't have to put up with their drama all day.

THE CONFESSIONAL: Fay, 34

In past unsuccessful relationships, which is how I spent my entire twenties, I always put my energy into supporting the guy. Now I'm paying the price for that and have to do all my identity work. I'm currently in this on-and-off relationship. We have "no plans" for each other, but never manage to cut off ties. It is the first time I started demanding my personal space. The current guy is a performer, literally and emotionally. And you know what? It's entertaining at first and I'm glad he has a creative persona and identity, but it's really annoying when you can't turn it off and it sucks my brains out without giving anything back. The guy just talks too much. It invades my space and leaves me with no energy to do my own projects.

2. Think Commitment Is for Squares

Okay, so marriage and commitment seem like an archaic institution. If you're like me, the very thought of being called a "wife" or saying "till death do us part" can make you break out in a cold sweat. But lest we get off topic here, don't forget this book isn't about marriage—it's about learning to sustain healthy, intimate relationships. While it's natural to worry about becoming "normal" or conventional, it's equally important to realize that there's no one blueprint for how you're supposed to act in a relationship. For example, every time I see a woman with drool on her shirt pushing a stroller down the street, I worry that I will become like her one day. But then I realize I wouldn't be like her, or anyone else for that matter. I would be *me* with a stroller. Or, on second thought, no stroller. Hell, maybe I'll just lug the tot around on my back all day.

Just because we view commitment as conventional, that doesn't mean we can't approach the matter more unconventionally. If you're too busy rebelling against social convention, you could end up forgoing things you might actually enjoy. I mean, tradition isn't all bad. You just need to toss the parts you hate and keep those you like. So instead of complaining about how prosaic it all is, why not use your creativity and passion to create a relationship and lifestyle that are unique and inspire you? And while it's great that you're an individual, it's okay to admit you may have some things in common with other people, like your need for companionship, support, and love. That doesn't make you square—it just makes you human.

3. Think They're Undateable

Many Free Spirits have it in their minds that they're somehow "undateable." No one's denying that artists, creative types, and independent thinkers can be notoriously difficult to live with. Can you imagine what it must have been like to shack up with Freud, Hemingway, or Nietzsche? But if these guys found someone who'd put up with them, you can, too. While it's true that some Free Spirits may be quite a handful, or even (dare I say it) a tad high-strung and dramatic, there's no reason why you can't find someone willing to put up with your zaniness.

Whether you come from a long line of uppity women or have seen your fair share of relationships spontaneously combust, there's no reason you can't have a perfectly satisfying relationship. Sure, you probably have your share of little eccentricities, such as

Kiss and Run

eating ice cream with a fork, laughing in your sleep, or walking your cat around the block on a leash. But find me one person who isn't crazy, weird, or strange in some way. No matter how much we deny it, all of us have bizarre quirks and issues that we try to hide from the world. As tempting as it is to hide behind your kookiness as a way of deliberately avoiding relationships, it will only hurt you in the end.

Unless you're biting the heads off chickens at home, your personality shouldn't commit you to a life of solitude. Some people actually enjoy a companion with a fiery, passionate side, provided you don't burn the house down during one of your moods. So while living with you won't be a walk in the park, it's hardly the minefield you make it out to be.

GET OVER IT: SUREFIRE STRATEGIES

Since you probably know your yin from your yang, I don't have to tell you that a little of both goes a long way. Spending your life in pursuit of a creative goal to the exclusion of everything else may seem noble, but what about your need for companionship? And even if you're not technically an *artiste* but love the freedom that constant change and self-exploration bring, you should realize that it's hardly an all-or-nothing proposition. After all, good relationships bring with them an immense capacity for learning and growth. So if you're finding that your free-spirited lifestyle is interfering with your romantic goals or that you've been using it as an excuse to avoid commitment, it's time you got some hard answers to your hard questions.

THE CONFESSIONAL: Hailey, 37

I feel smothered whenever I sense that anything is permanent—and that goes for jobs as well as men. I guess I enjoy uncertainty. Partially, it's my nature to be restless. I need a lot more excitement than most

Elina Furman

people, and settling down is not conducive to excitement. I am so fear-ful of being tied down that I can't even commit to buying furniture. I have worked abroad several times, and I like to know that I can be ready for the next international assignment quickly. Basically, I want to know that I can pack up and run in less than a week. I fear boredom and a "normal" life above all else.

Q. *"I'm pretty free-spirited and fun, but something happens when I get into a relationship. I stop going out as much, don't take as many chances, and even become depressed, regardless of how well things are going. What do I do?"*

A. Look, we've all been there. You're sitting around with your guy after a long day of work and then it starts: "So what do you want to do?" "I don't know, what do you want to do?" And so on and so on, until one of you runs out of the room screaming from the sheer banality of it all.

As a Free Spirit, you get off on the idea of unlimited possibilities and constant change. You want to be able to evolve and to be spontaneous, and you worry that a committed relationship will end any possibility of reinvention. While most unions tend to devolve into staleness from time to time, it's not an inevitability.

If you're wondering why relationships always leave you so drained, you might want to take a good hard look at yourself. While some guys are truly less exciting than others, taking accountability for your own lackluster relationship performance can only help matters. The reason so many Free Spirits are scared stiff of commitment is because they're more likely to act in conventional ways once they've made one. "How's that?" you ask. Well, it's usually the people who fear boredom most who end up setting up habits and routines in relationships. So once they're sufficiently bored, they can use the dullness excuse to hightail it out of there.

Many of us, Free Spirits included, have these presuppositions about what being in a relationship involves. Maybe we saw our parents trapped in traditional gender roles. Maybe we've read books where one person (most likely the woman) has to sacrifice more than her partner. Whatever the reason, even Free Spirits like you have been known to willingly give up their hobbies, interests, and goals in order to act out whatever idea they have of a girlfriend or wife, at least for a little while. But once that identity becomes restrictive, you blame the guy and the relationship for the problem, when it was really you who gave up on yourself. In a way, it's a self-perpetuating cycle that prevents you from wanting to commit in the future.

If you tend to get stuck in relationship ruts, realize it's because you impose these barriers on yourself. There's no reason you can't be as courageous, fiery, and adventurous as you were in your single days. The most important consideration is to continue living the life you did when you were single, while maintaining your bonds. It may seem like a tall order, but you'd be surprised at how doable it is, especially if you're with a guy who appreciates your million and one quirks and eccentricities. After all, that's why he fell in love with you in the first place. If you give those up, you're actually giving up on the relationship. So instead of viewing your personal and relationship interests as incompatible, think of one as serving the other. If you're doing what makes you happy and pursuing your interests, you will be happier, your partner will be happier, and your relationship will thrive—simple as that.

The Free Spirit Manifesto

Think you can't be your usual zany self and still be in a committed relationship? Think again. All you need to do is pledge to uphold the bylaws of free-spiritedness. While this may make you a bad little homemaker, it will make you a fundamentally more interesting and vital partner. And when it comes down to it, how would you rather be remembered?

- I will not freak out about dirty socks on the floor nor put them away.
- I will find an alternative work space when I need time to be alone.
- I will learn the art of making reservations and getting take-out.
- I will give myself an hour of uninterrupted time to play every day.
- I will talk to a stranger every day.
- I will continue to go to movies and events by myself.
- I will take a mini-vacation alone or with my friends once a year.
- I will continue to take classes and try new things.
- I will not cancel plans with my friends even though I'm feeling lazy.

THE CONFESSIONAL: Cory, 29

My outward character—socially, creatively, and professionally—is defined to some degree by my flightiness when it comes to relationships. The older I get and the more relationships I have, the more I realize how nearly impossible it would be for me to find someone whom I could truly be happy with. I am an aspiring writer and have felt stagnant for the last two years. I believe there is a connection—I am very protective of my aspirations and don't like to talk about my career (or lack thereof these days). I also feel that I would need to be more established and stable in my writing before I could be in a committed relationship. It would be very hard for me to share that aspect of my life with someone else, but at the same time, I am extremely engrossed internally with my creative prospects, to the point where I can never really disconnect. It is a source of enormous conflict that is nearly impossible to communicate. Maybe I will feel differently if and when I have more success. I don't want to be alone for the rest of my life, but I think that I need to accomplish certain things for myself, by myself, before I can be open to that kind of intimacy.

Q. *"My photography is all about loneliness, pain, and despair. I don't really see how I can still capture all those feelings in my work if I'm happily involved in a relationship."*

A. Just because you're suffering doesn't mean you can produce great art. If that were the case, every depressed person would be an artistic genius. So the reverse also applies: just because you're a talented artist doesn't mean you have to suffer all the time.

I'm sure you've had enough traumas and dramas in your life to draw on—you don't have to keep reenacting the same sad scenarios. While you may be inspired to portray those experiences in your creative work, your life can be a much rosier picture. After all, many writers and artists use empathy as a way to create characters or relate to their subjects. Not everything has to be autobiographical. If it did, artists would never have the time to make any work—they'd always be off somewhere living one crazy adventure after another.

On the contrary, many successful artists report that being in a stable and fulfilling relationship has inspired and improved their work, giving them more creative footing in the long run. In the end, the idea of sacrificing and suffering for one's creative goals may be a popular concept, but don't underestimate the power of happiness, either.

THE CONFESSIONAL: Paula, 41

Ever since I was three years old I was painting on walls, tables, anything I could get my hands on. It's always been my thing. Being a painter is a major part of my self-concept and identity, and I've always known I would be painting all my life, whether I was successful or not. Throughout my twenties, I had many different relationships, but I always kept my work guarded and was scared about getting seriously involved with anyone. I thought I would have to somehow choose be-

Elina Furman

tween work and having a family. When I met Vince, my husband, my productivity definitely dropped off. I stopped painting as much and was just enjoying starting our life together. But now that we have two kids, I really have to go out of my way to create a mental and physical space so I can paint. And while it's hard, it's definitely doable. We set aside room in the den for me to work. I also make sure to paint in the morning after the kids are off to school, and I have become great at scheduling. It also helps to turn off all the phones and TV and give myself a distraction-free zone. Absolutely no calls while I'm working. And when my husband comes home from work, he takes care of the kids for a few hours so I can get my work done. It's helped that he understands me and values what I do.

Q. *"My mom gave up her career, and I know tons of other women who are just too busy with work and raising families to follow through on their passions. How do I know I won't end up like them?"*

A. Balancing relationships, family, and creative goals can be extremely difficult. After all, Michelangelo didn't have to do the cooking and Beethoven never had to take out the trash. And the women artists who did succeed in the past were either independently wealthy, had supportive husbands, or started late in life, once their kids were grown. But let's face it—while Mom may have liked her work, she may have actually enjoyed staying home more. And as for the other women, how do you know they were as motivated and driven as you are? You have no idea about the factors that contributed to their decisions.

Many times women say they gave something up for their families or husbands when in fact they had their own issues to deal with. Maybe they didn't think they were talented enough, maybe they got tired of living in a hut with no running water, or maybe the act of putting pen to paper or brush to canvas every day just got too strenuous. When it comes to measuring how driven we are, the proof is really in the pudding. So if there's no productivity or motivation, the work must not have been that important.

So how do you know if you'll end up like them? Well, you don't. There is no certainty or guarantee that a relationship won't undermine your personal life goals and that you will remain productive in your chosen field—unless, of course, you're truly motivated. In that case, there's very little that can come between you and your life calling, since you'll fight tooth and nail to get the time and space you need to produce. It's really up to you. After all, very few partners will ever tell you to stop doing what makes you happy. And if they do, well, then you don't want them in the first place.

The following are some other internal blocks that some of you Free Spirits will face.

- **Laziness.** We're all guilty of it, yet very few of us admit to ever being that way. Isn't it much easier to let your guy distract you with a humorous account of his day than to slog into your dark office or make the long drive to your cooking classes? No one's saying it's easy, but what really distinguishes one productive person from another is discipline. Getting up early every day, spending a few hours toiling over your work, cutting out all distractions, and focusing on the task at hand is the only way to stay motivated every single day.

- **Perfectionism.** Since many artists are perfectionists, it's only normal that you want to be the perfect wife, girlfriend, or partner. But this trait can be a huge impediment to both your creativity and your personal life. When it comes to your projects, it can stifle the creative process and make you self-conscious. And when it comes to your personal life, it can lead you to expend maximum energy at all times, attempting to do everything in the best possible way and feeling guilty because you haven't done any of them well enough. While it's normal to want to try to do everything well, it can lead to burnout and even less energy to devote to your pursuits.

- **Isolation.** Many women report feeling creatively isolated after moving in with their partner, relocating to another city, or losing a job. But just because you've lost your old support network doesn't mean you can't set up a new one. Finding mentors, new friends, and a community of like-minded people is a great way to stay active in your chosen field. Not only will it keep you motivated, it will allow you to learn how other women balance the Free Spirit/relationship conundrum. Whether you take an art class, find activity partners in your local paper, or join a community theater, the act of feeding your independent spirit day after day will serve as a constant reminder of your core passions and identity.

FREE SPIRIT RECAP

No one is saying you're flaky or can't get through one chapter before flying off on some madcap adventure, but here's a quick synopsis of what you may have missed.

- While following your bliss and being creative may be noble causes, so is your love life.

- Dating needy and possessive men who make excessive demands on your time is a sure way to develop commitment anxiety.

- While it's great that you're so unconventional, it's okay to admit you may have some things in common with other people, such as your need for companionship, support, and love.

- The idea of sacrificing and suffering for one's creative goals may be a popular concept, but don't underestimate the power of happiness, either.

- By dating guys who don't fit the "alternative" mold, you may find that you're able to put even more energy and effort into your creative outlets when you don't have to put up with their drama all day.

- While it's natural to worry about becoming "normal" or conventional, it's equally important to realize that there's no one blueprint for how you're supposed to act in a relationship.

- You may be quite a handful, but there's no reason why you can't find someone willing to put up with your zaniness.

- It's usually the people who fear boredom most who end up setting up habits and routines in relationships.

- A true Free Spirit is someone who is unafraid. After all, it takes a lot of courage to commit and be intimate with one person.

7

Damsel in Distress

$\mathcal{S}$top me if you've heard any of these before:

Q. How does a man show he's planning for the future?
A. He buys two cases of beer instead of one.

Q. What do men and mascara have in common?
A. They both run at the first sign of emotion.

Q. What do men and sperm have in common?
A. They both have a one-in-a-million chance of becoming a human being.

Tsk, tsk, tsk.

Okay, so he lied. He didn't call. He cheated. He left you at the altar. He used your international calling card. He slept with your best friend. There're a gazillion things that he may have done wrong, but are *all* men really that bad? And are you really such a helpless victim?

When it comes to relationships, all of us, both women and men, have done the walking-wounded thing. We've suffered our share of bad breakups, dashed hopes, and major disappointment. But does that mean you should roll over, brand yourself a victim, and never get out there again?

Having heard one too many times that men are such evil, disgusting, smelly jerks and women are these perfect, innocent beings who are forced to share the same planet with them, I would like to take this opportunity to say, *"Stop!"* I can't help bristling at these rampant gender-alizations. While there are no doubt some bad apples of the XY persuasion, can we honestly say there are not just as many women who fit that criterion? As funny and harmless as these jokes seem, man-hating, bashing, and criticizing are no laughing matter. In fact, they reveal far more about us as women than we would ever care to admit.

The Damsel in Distress is someone who's given up on the prospect of men, dating, and finding love. Whether it's because of a divorce, difficulties in childhood, a painful breakup, or abuse, she's usually been hurt in some way and has difficulty trusting. While some Damsels tend to think that all men are basically crap and choose to blow off the whole dating scene altogether, others continue to date but worry that making a commitment can only lead to further turmoil.

When it comes to the Damsels of this world, the key word here is *fear*.

- You fear that you will be rejected.
- You fear that you are never going to find someone to love you.
- You fear exposing your true self to a partner only to be disappointed when he turns out to be a jerk.
- You fear that you are too needy.
- You fear you have nothing left to give in a relationship.
- You fear you have become too jaded and cynical.
- You fear being abandoned again.
- You fear you are never going to get over your last relationship.
- You fear that you're unlovable.

THE CONFESSIONAL: Gale, 27

My best friend, whom I could have totally seen myself with long-term, wanted to start dating. We had been friends for a while. I could tell him anything and spend all my time with him and never get bored. He's an amazing guy, brilliant, witty, an incredible cook. He had this uncanny

> *ability to make me feel special and beautiful, but was always honest and forthcoming with me. Yet I was really scared about entertaining the idea of us becoming more because the realization that he could potentially be "the one" freaked me out. And I also feared the possibility that he wouldn't really be able to love me. I distrust men, and I'm not entirely sure where this stems from. My mother passed away when I was 16. I don't perceive life as permanent and things as everlasting, and yet I get frustrated by the lack of permanence and substance in my relationships. Things that are meaningful and substantial should ideally last forever, and yet they don't.*

To Damsels, the search for love has become nothing more than a recipe for heartbreak, which is why they tend to avoid men and relationships rather than taking a chance on love. But all their talk about men being inscrutable, confusing, and downright obnoxious is really just a façade that keeps them from opening up to new people. They simply do not want to lay their all-too-human flaws and vulnerabilities open for inspection. And if that means avoiding getting involved for as long as possible, then so be it. Damsels figure, "I've been hurt, cheated on, and abused. There's no way I'm getting into another relationship," and use their pain and emotional turmoil to shield themselves from commitment.

In the end, when it comes to your relationships or lack thereof, it's all about taking responsibility. While no one's disputing that you've ended up with some questionable men or had some bad things happen to you, glossing over your own personal flaws, issues, and hang-ups can prevent you from taking accountability for your actions and examining what your choices say about your own deeply buried commitment fears. So if you can't think of even one thing you did to contribute to your relationship problems, think harder! After all, it's easier to go on believing that your fear of commitment has to do with the fact that men are jerks than to actually stop and think about why you picked them, fed them, and housed them in the first place.

THE DOCTOR IS IN

The first thing to do is to embrace your issues. Awareness is key. If somebody has been hiding behind different excuses as to why they can't have a relationship or blaming it on the guy, then they are not going to be able to deal with the issues. But if you can say, "Hey, I'm the one who's afraid of committing because I'm afraid of getting dumped, abandoned, and hurt. My flaws will be seen, and then I'll be embarrassed or shamed," then embrace that. If you can admit that, then there's room to make changes.

—*Debra Mandel, Ph.D.*

QUIZ: ARE YOU A DAMSEL IN DISTRESS?

We all have our share of battle wounds. You'd be hard pressed to find anyone who's escaped the dating world unscathed. It's just a question of how deep your issues run and whether you've allowed them to affect your outlook on commitment and relationships. Since we all have the Damsel complex to some degree, take this quiz to find where you fall on the Damsel meter.

1. **When you see a couple holding hands and kissing on the street, you think:**

   A. Ugh, how annoying! I give them two weeks.

   B. They're probably on their third date.

   C. Awww, how sweet.

2. **You're on a date with a really cool guy and it's going really well. He's funny and charming, and he asks you lots of questions about yourself. Then a hot girl walks by and you notice him sneaking a peek. You think:**

   A. What a jerk! He's just like the rest of them.

   B. He probably thinks she's prettier than me.

   C. I wonder where she bought that blouse.

3. **What's your opinion of your ex-boyfriend?**
   A. Just your typical man—a compulsive liar, cheater, and jerk.
   B. He definitely had some issues.
   C. He was a good guy, but it just didn't work out between us.

4. **Finish this sentence: "All men are . . ."**
   A. Jerks!
   B. Just too complicated.
   C. I don't like stereotyping all men into one category.

5. **You've been seeing a guy for a couple of weeks now. He said he would call you at eight, but the phone doesn't ring all night. You think:**
   A. He's definitely cheating on me.
   B. He doesn't care about me.
   C. He probably just got busy and will call me tomorrow. I hope he's all right.

6. **You've just been promoted and even got a nice raise. What do you attribute your success to?**
   A. Sheer luck. I don't know how that happened.
   B. My ability to trick others into thinking I actually know what I'm doing.
   C. My hard work and talent.

7. **Your ex-boyfriend, who dumped you in a brief e-mail with no warning, calls you to let you know he's getting married. You:**
   A. Hope that he and his new bride have a great life . . . in hell!
   B. Muster up fake congratulations, but secretly feel like he's rubbing it in.
   C. Feel a slight twinge of discomfort but congratulate him nonetheless.

8. **Looking back on your relationship history, how many times have you been hurt?**
   A. All the time. I'm a jerk magnet.
   B. Pretty often.
   C. No more than anyone else.

9. **Your best friend and her boyfriend of three months get into a fight. When she calls you for advice, you suggest:**
   A. That they break up. It's never going to work out anyway, so she should dump him now.
   B. That she should look at the fight as a sign that something isn't right in the relationship.
   C. Encourage her to relax and try to see the matter from his point of view as well.

10. **When a friend compliments you on your new outfit, you:**
    A. Wonder if she's just trying to butter you up for a favor.
    B. Say, "What, this old thing?"
    C. Respond with a thank-you and a smile.

Scoring: To calculate your final score, assign a point value to each answer: 3 for every A, 2 for every B, and 1 for every C. Now add it all up and see where you rank.

23–30 Points: Cry Me a River

I'd feel sorry for you, but it seems that you've got the self-pity angle covered. You're probably tired of going through one bad experience after another and have resigned yourself to the idea that being alone is better than being with some jackass. While I can't disagree with you there, I definitely take offense at your line of reasoning. Just because you've happened to date one too many jerks in your time, that doesn't mean *all* men are that way. In the end, you might just be picking these mongrels to confirm your bad opinion of men because you're scared to commit. Have you ever thought of that?

 THE CONFESSIONAL: Yvonne, 32

Commitment-phobia plays a part in all of my relationships. I am deathly afraid of committing because I know that he will eventually cheat on me. My first boyfriend cheated on me repeatedly. I have a very hard time trusting guys I date. I turn into a psycho girlfriend. I try to not act jealous or suspicious, but it's hard.

Elina Furman

15–22 Points: A Case of Damselitis

When it comes to emotional baggage, you're packing one too many suitcases, lady. Maybe you've been hurt before. Who hasn't? Maybe you've been dumped. Welcome to the dating world. While no one would begrudge you a good pity party now and then, your natural tendency to nurse your wounds and hole up in your apartment for days isn't the best way of dealing with dating debacles. While it's good to deal with your anger, holding unnecessary grudges against the opposite sex and feeling bad about yourself can make you reluctant to commit to a good relationship when it does come along.

14 or Fewer Points: More Diva than Damsel

You're definitely a lot more diva than damsel. Like the rest of us, you've had your share of personal setbacks, but you're not about to let those experiences color the way you look at yourself, the world, or your relationships. After all, it takes two to tango, and as much as you want to blame the men in your life, you accept responsibility for your part as well. You've probably learned from your mistakes, forgiven the ogres in your life, and moved on with renewed confidence.

DAMSEL PROTESTS: "I'M NOT A DAMSEL IN DISTRESS, I'M JUST . . ."

For some of you, a relationship is probably right down there with a root canal on your list of must-haves. If so, then I won't have to convince you that you have your share of commitment woes. Yet some of you may not be aware of your issues. You may be completely oblivious to the internal negativity that is sabotaging your chances for a real honest-to-goodness commitment. So whether you're resigned to a life alone or are desperately seeking a union that keeps eluding you, check out some of these common Damsel protests.

1. **"I'm Just Tired of Dating."** I hear you. All those hours logged cuddling, talking about the future, and putting up with annoying quirks and habits—and not a thing to show for it. You probably put a lot of energy and effort into your last relationship, and when it didn't work out as planned, it's fair to say

there was some disappointment and one too many nights singing Alanis Morissette's "You Oughta Know."

There is nothing worse than feeling like all that hard work you invested in someone was a colossal waste of time. So is it any surprise that the last thing you want to do is start dating again? Talk about an exercise in futility. You have to dress up, style your hair, get your nails done, come up with witty repartee, hire a babysitter . . . a million and one things. And once you drag yourself out of the house, there are no guarantees of connection or chemistry. Suddenly, even watching a VH1 marathon of back-to-back *Surreal Life* episodes can seem more appealing than dating.

It's easy for Damsels to get caught up in this line of thinking. While Serial Daters tend to overdate, some Damsels tend to underdate and suffer from home-alone syndrome. Of course, no one would dispute that all relationships are hard work and often require a huge investment without a guaranteed return, but that doesn't mean they're not worth it. Just because your first date doesn't translate to a second or your relationship didn't result in a long-term commitment, that doesn't mean it was a failure. In fact, you probably ended up learning a lot about yourself and what you want from the next relationship. So while I wouldn't advise you to run amuck racking up all the dating points you can, it's important to turn off the TV, put down your knitting needles, and try to get out of the house at least once in while.

THE CONFESSIONAL: Maureen, 30

I was hurt very badly in a relationship about three years ago. I loved him dearly. He was protective of me and I felt he looked out for me. We had wonderful conversations; he was very intelligent and funny, very clever. It seemed that the depth of physical attraction went both ways. I truly enjoyed every moment I spent with him. He asked me to move in with him about five months into the relationship. I have never lived

> with a man, not even my ex-fiancé. I did give it some thought but said no, because I don't want to live with a man until I am married. As much as I loved him, I didn't think it was a smart thing to do. A few weeks later he broke up with me with no explanation whatsoever. I was depressed for a long time afterward. I couldn't eat at all, and every time I woke from sleeping, I realized it wasn't a nightmare, he really wasn't with me, and I would begin to cry. It was very hard. He has tried to contact me a few times over the last three years. He asked to see me to talk to me but stood me up. I did finally see him again and I didn't get anything out of it. He really didn't have much to say—no apology, still no reason. Didn't say he wanted me back, nothing.

2. "I'm Just Still Hung Up on My Last Relationship."
Whether you (a) despise your ex and want nothing more than to see his mug shot on the five o'clock news, (b) still love him desperately despite the fact that he slept with your cousin, or (c) both of the above, moving on from a past relationship can be an excruciating process. It's all too easy for Damsels to get stuck in the past. But living in the past is one of the easiest ways to avoid commitment in the present.

Who cares if he abandoned you in your hour of need? Who cares if he never once offered to pay his share of dinner? Suddenly, all the bad things he did stop mattering and all the problems the two of you had are swept under the rug until all you can think about are those special twinkly moments when everything seemed perfectly preordained by the love gods.

Some commitment-phobes tend to overromanticize their former relationships for one simple reason—it keeps them from having to make new commitments in the present. After all, if you're too busy romanticizing a past relationship, there's really no way you'll end up in a new relationship, which is precisely the point. If no one measures up to your perfect ex-boyfriend (and since he is a fantasy, no one will ever quite cut it), you can stay single and never face up to your fears of connecting with someone new.

Conversely, some of you get stuck in the past by demonizing your exes and blowing their faults all out of proportion. But holding on to your anger is just another way of holding on to your ex and can prevent you from entering new relationships. Either way, whether you romanticize or demonize your exes, you'll have to get over the past if you want to have any hope of making another commitment.

3. **"I'm Just Scared of Ending Up Like My Parents."** If your parents are divorced, trapped in an unloving marriage, or just plain nutcases, they have probably colored the way you look at commitment. It's entirely normal to dread the prospect of turning into your parents. Some of you would rather die than marry a man like your dad, and others of you are dreadfully afraid of ending up like your mother. You think, "My parents are so screwed up, so it's not my fault that I'm having all these problems." Or, "Why even try if I'm just going to end up like them anyway?"

It should come as no surprise, then, that Damsels tend to come from broken homes and dysfunctional families. A large percentage of women with commitment issues have had early traumas in their families, whether it's divorce, abuse, abandonment, or the death of a parent. And while none of us can ever fully escape our family legacy, it's important that we try to keep the good, leave the bad, and embrace our heritage rather than deny it. For instance, while an easily excitable nature may have made your mom go berserk at the slightest provocation, you can take control of your own high-strung personality by taking up a highly competitive hobby. Or if you're constantly finding yourself attracted to passive and wounded guys like your dad, find another outlet for your Florence Nightingale tendencies by volunteering at a local animal shelter.

It may be perfectly normal to worry about ending up like your parents or marrying a parental clone, but there's no sense in thinking that you are doomed to repeat all their mistakes. After all, genetics are hardly an excuse for avoiding commitment.

Elina Furman

THE CONFESSIONAL: Joy, 46

Because of the way I was raised, I have often chosen people who were abusive. Having dated abusers, losers, alcoholics, addicts, drunks, and crazy people, I've been out there trying to fix my family for a lot of years, which is the idea behind growing up in a dysfunctional family. We tend to internalize what goes on, and years later we are choosing mates where we are subconsciously working on stuff with our family. I didn't have a model for healthy relationships, so it made it difficult to learn what the boundaries are, what it's like to have a healthy relationship. My inability to make good choices was so far up in my face that I needed to go into therapy to figure out what would lead me to choose to be with someone like that. Relationship trauma has been a recurrent theme in my life, but I've brought a lot of it on myself because of my conditioning. I'm in the process of learning how to transform all that into something positive.

TOP DAMSEL IN DISTRESS HANG-UPS

Look, we've all made mistakes. Even if you did nothing wrong in the relationship (except pick him in the first place) and are truly a victim, your one mistake moving forward would be to continue acting like one. It may be easy to get caught in the "poor me" mentality, but it can also make you more commitment-phobic in the long run. So while you may have fallen into a negative mental spiral, that doesn't mean you can't work your way out of it. Here are some of the most common ways Damsels get hung up.

1. Worrying About Getting Hurt

Love hurts. Love sucks. Relationships take hard work. What else is new? While being single definitely has advantages—like watching whatever you want on TV, not having to call in when you're late, and never using the insufferable word *we*—it can be very addictive for all the same reasons. Staying single is safe and doesn't challenge you to get out of your comfort zone. After all, as great as it feels, falling in love can be terrifying. There are no guarantees, no promises, and no safe cushion to land on when things go bust. But while avoiding commitment may keep you in a safe cocoon of late-night television, it can also keep you from finding happiness.

If your commitment-phobia is deeply rooted in the fear that you'll get hurt again, there's hope for you yet. Whether you've stopped dating altogether or just have a negative attitude about the prospect of finding someone good enough to commit to, you'll need to relax and realize that all of us have that fear. Breaking up hurts—so what? Does that mean you're going to lock yourself in a nunnery? After all, what's the worst that can happen?

A. You cry yourself to sleep for a few months.
B. You lose or gain weight.
C. You feel mopey and have a hard time concentrating.
D. You pester all your friends and family members with daily "why me?" phone calls.

When you really break it down, heartbreak isn't fatal—it just feels like it is. And what's so horrible about the feeling of loss anyway? At least it's an emotion. Would you rather shut down and not feel anything at all? You've probably been through a lot of difficult experiences in your life, and you've managed to cope and come out even stronger because of them. So instead of worrying about heartache, laugh boldly in its face and just say, "Bring it on!"

THE DOCTOR IS IN

When it comes to relationships, it's important not to care so much about the outcome. We don't have control over whether a relationship works out or not. So we have to let go of the need for our relationships to have a certain outcome and instead be centered and grounded enough within ourselves to say, "I want to give it a shot anyway, whether it works out or not." It's important to adopt the "better to have loved and lost then never to have loved at all" philosophy.

—*Debra Mandel, Ph.D.*

Elina Furman

VICTIM OR VIXEN?

If it's all going to end disastrously, why even try—right? Acting like a victim can be oh so draining. It can leave you feeling hopeless and even lead you to blow off perfectly good opportunities, whether it's jobs, parties, or men. Problem is, if you expect to be disappointed, you probably will be. Attitude is the main element that separates the victims from the vixens. Still having trouble figuring out which vibe you give off? Check out the key differences:

VIXEN	VICTIM
Hosts cocktail parties	Hosts pity parties
Dates once a week	Dates once in a lifetime
Falls from grace	Falls on her face
Thinks chivalry is cute	Thinks chivalry is dead
Weekend warrior	Weekend snoozer
Is gossip	Starts gossip
Cyber sex	Cyber rants
Loves compliments	Loves to complain
Makes a move	Misses a move
Thinks life is too short to feel bad	Thinks life is too short
Takes credit for her success	Attributes success to luck

THE CONFESSIONAL: Nadine, 34

My parents fought all the time. I would duck dishes at the dinner table that my dad would throw. They got divorced when I was 13, and I didn't speak to him for a couple of years. I guess my commitment issues have to do with trust. I haven't met somebody I could feel very close to. I don't really trust anyone. I know that every guy I've ever met has dropped the ball at some point or another, and I know that I'm never going to disappoint myself. The more I know men, the less I like them and their mentalities. So why even get involved?

2. Pointing Fingers

We live in a culture of male-bashing, female-patronizing, and gender-dividing. Walk into any bookstore and you'll find a glut of books telling you how much better or different women are from men. But the one we really need is *Men Aren't the Enemy and Women Aren't Perfect*. Or how about *Men and Women Are Both from Planet Earth*?

While hearing about what a goddess you are and how he never truly deserved you may seem empowering at first, this kind of simplistic, divisive drivel can lead to more problems in the long run. Or what about the constant harangues on how men and women speak two different languages? It may be a good excuse for why you have so much trouble communicating with men, but this line of thought only creates more conflict between the sexes.

Gender-alizations are especially troubling because they make you think that every relationship problem occurs because men and women are from different planets: "Oh, that's why that never worked out!" "Oh, that's why he was such a prick." This line of thinking completely absolves you of any personal responsibility. And Damsels tend to buy in to these notions, more so than others.

While men and women do have differences, the last time I checked we both spoke English (some of us better than others) and have the same basic human needs for food, warmth, companionship, and shelter. And while it's true that men and women can vary in their communication styles, focusing on that gap can make us even more intolerant of men, wanting to throw our hands up in the air and forget the whole business.

The truth is that differences exist in every relationship—with your friends, your parents, and your siblings. None of us is exactly alike, but our differences exist from person to person, not just from men to women. In the end, it takes two people to turn a relationship from sweet to sour. So if you're too busy focusing on what he did wrong and how perfect you are, you probably will never find out all the ways in which you yourself sabotaged the relationship. Until you stop believing that men are an alien subspecies who don't deserve to breathe the

Elina Furman

same air as you, you'll continue to act out the commitment-phobic patterns by choosing the very types of men who'll confirm your negative worldview.

THE CONFESSIONAL: Carrie, 38

I say men don't want to be with me and don't want to commit, but I'm the one who leaves the relationship. My dad was kind of abusive, but I've never been with an abusive man. I would choose passive, codependent men who idolize me and put me at the center of their universe. My marriage was all about me. It was all about making sure I was taken care of. The second long-term relationship was like that, too. The guy absolutely went above and beyond in terms of taking care of me. But I'm the one who ends them. In my last relationship, I was so emotionally abusive to him. I really, really broke his heart when I broke up with him. He ended up being able to open up to me and love me unconditionally. I didn't feel worthy of it, so I kind of sabotaged the whole relationship.

WHY YOU'RE A JERK, TOO

Yeah, yeah. I know, you're perfect. Now what? The truth is, no one is perfect. No, not even you. No matter how many times you think men have wronged you, you're not going to get over your commitment issues by laying all the blame on men. Remember that time you acted like a birthday Nazi when he got you the wrong gift? Or the time you freaked out when he forgot to pick up something at the store? See, not so perfect, are you? Not to be mean or anything, but once you admit that you're human and have flaws just like everyone else, you can stop the victim cycle once and for all. Check off each statement that applies to you.

- I've dissed a guy in front of his friends.
- I purposely didn't call a guy when I said I would.
- I broke up with someone by phasing him out rather than by being totally honest.

- I've smugly rejected a guy when he approached to ask me out.
- I've cheated on a boyfriend/husband.
- I've made fun of a date behind his back with my friends.
- I've held out sexually to get my way.
- I forgot to call when I said I would.
- I've yelled and lost my temper in the heat of the moment.
- I've lied to my dates when they asked if I was seeing other people.
- I've canceled a date with a guy when a better offer came along.
- I've flirted with other guys in front of my date.
- I've yelled at a boyfriend for talking to other girls.
- I've showed up drunk on a date.
- I've disappeared for two weeks without so much as a phone call.
- I've pretended to leave my wallet at home when it was time to pay.
- I've emotionally manipulated men to get my way.
- I've dated someone for superficial reasons (rich, attractive, connected, etc.).

3. Denying You Want a Commitment

We've all heard about Bridget Jones's "Smug Marrieds," those pesky couples who can't fathom how anyone survives without a partner or a salad spinner. But now we have a new breed of smug people, the "Smug Singles"—women who would rather shop for shoes than a husband. Some of these women really do prefer the freedom and opportunity to make out with whomever, whenever they want. However, many others are not entirely convinced. Many are so scared that a committed relationship is not in the cards that they perform this pseudo-empowerment trick by telling themselves they don't want one in the first place.

Some of you may be so terrified of getting hurt that you've convinced yourself that you actually don't want a committed relationship. Many Damsels put on a "single front," training themselves not to want things because of the chance they won't get them. And while it's true that some of you may not want a committed relationship, there are definitely others of you who fear that you'll end up alone, and so you turn the tables by telling yourself you wouldn't have it any other way.

"I'm just not the marrying kind," "I don't need love to feel complete," "I've always been a loner"—you've probably convinced yourself of at least one of these. The problem is that after hearing yourself say over and over that you don't want a relationship, you'll probably start to believe it. Eventually your family, friends, and dates will start to believe it, too. Everyone will think, "Oh, that Elina. She'll never settle down." And that will be that. You will have escalated your commitment to noncommitment, so even when (or if) you do change your mind, you will feel obligated to follow through on your word. Worst of all, after telling yourself you really couldn't care less about relationships, you may actually stop caring at all.

4. Oh No You Didn't!

We've all seen those hysterically funny personal ads where the online daters go on and on about what they *don't* want in a relationship. If you thought having a long list of demands was bad enough, then the list of don'ts is even worse. It's the same as the shopping list from hell found in the Nitpicker chapter, but in reverse. Not only do you sound like you've been through your share of bad dates and relationships (and who wants to get involved with someone with such a huge chip on her shoulder?), focusing on what you don't want is the surest way to get precisely that. You see, it's really a matter of perspective. Think about the positive, and that's all you'll see. Focus on the negative, and suddenly it's all around you. So if your list of don'ts runs anything like the one below, you may end up scaring off perfectly great men and attracting the very types you're looking to avoid. When in doubt, here's an easy way to flip your script.

DONT'S	DOS
No druggies	Healthy lifestyle
No arrogant jerks	Quiet confidence
No psychopaths	Relatively sane
No cheaters	Loyalty
No liars	Honesty
No deadbeats	Hardworking
No mama's boys	Independent
No meat-eaters	Environmentally conscious
No passive-aggressives	Direct communicator

THE CONFESSIONAL: Kara, 37

There is a long list of what I don't want. Here goes: no druggies, liars, codependents, adult children of whatever, idiots, arrogant bastards, perverts, foot fetishists, closet homosexuals, psychopaths, bipolars, compulsive spenders, criminals, sports fanatics, cheaters, midlife-crisis jackasses, mama's boys, extreme extroverts, guru types, daddy figures, or slovenly, unclean men.

GET OVER IT: SUREFIRE STRATEGIES

For damsels, the road to recovery is hardly an easy one. There's no instant cure for the host of complicated feelings leading you to avoid commitment. While I would never want you to spiral into a negative pattern of assuming all your relationship problems are somehow your fault, it's important that you recognize what role, if any, you played in this sorry state of events. Continuing to act out these behavior cycles while claiming that you want a solid, committed relationship may seem like a nifty little trick, but as you've probably guessed, I'm on to you! The question is: are you really ready to look at what's keeping you from making a commitment?

> **Q. "It sounds a lot like you're blaming the victim here. As a self-professed Damsel, I can't see how it's my fault that I've been burned in love so many times."**

A. We've all been on the receiving end of bad behavior and some downright foul antics. There's the time my first high-school boyfriend broke up with me. Devastating! And then there was my sophomore year in college, when I slept with my friendly next-door psycho, who thought it was cute to parade other girls in front of me. Nightmare! Of course, looking back, it's not like I can claim to have been an angel or anything. I've done plenty of shady stuff in my day and am well aware that I can't spend my life blaming men for all my problems. When it comes down to it, for every bad thing that has happened with men, I can think of three or four guys that rocked my world.

In life and love, a few bad experiences are par for the course. We've all been dealt some hard blows and may even have been humbled in the process. But how often is this happening to you? If you responded with "all the time," then a little introspection could be just what the shrink ordered. If you don't want to take responsibility, fine. If you want to blame all your problems on the evil Y chromosome, fine. That's your choice. But if the same thing keeps happening again and again, it would only make sense to analyze the pattern.

1. **Did you let others cross your boundaries?** There are plenty of ways that someone could cross the line. There's crashing at your place after a night of hard drinking with his friends, not showing up when he says he will, and flirting with other people in front of you. Boundaries are tricky: if you don't have clear ones outlined in the beginning of a relationship, expect to have them trespassed. But it's not entirely men's fault, either. All of us, men *and* women, will always try to get away with as much as possible. It's our way of testing the waters to see what each one of us is made of. So while you can blame men all you want, it's your job to guard your turf and make sure no one steps out of line.

2. **Did you communicate your needs?** We women are funny when it comes to communication. We're always going on and on about how important it is, how men can't share their feelings, how superior we are in that department. But when we get mad, our best effort at communication boils down to the silent treatment with the occasional dramatic sigh thrown in for good measure. Yeah, sure, *that's* effective! Think back to your own relationships. Did you clearly state what you did and did not like? Did you point out that his forgetting to call you

pisses you off? Did you make sure to spell out that coming home drunk every night was a deal breaker? After all, you can't blame the men in your life if you didn't follow through on your part of the communication gap.

3. **Did you settle for less than you deserved?** While Nitpickers tend to ask for the world on a platter, Damsels often ask for a nibble on a paper plate. If your idea of a great guy has boiled down to (a) disease-free, (b) no prior arrest record, and (c) comes over once a month, it may be time to upgrade your list of requirements. Of course, no one's telling you to come up with a mile-long list of nitpicky demands, but if you're constantly settling for someone who isn't respectful, honest, or caring, don't be surprised to find yourself always disappointed.

4. **Did you ignore the signs?** When it comes to jerks, it's not too hard to pick one out of a crowd. There he goes now, making lewd gestures at the girl walking by and hitting his retired parents up for more money. Of course, some jerks start out great—putting on the charm, wooing you with abandon, and telling you how wonderful you are. Once you're hooked, the jerk in sheep's clothing comes out, and by then it's too late to do anything about it. The one thing you have to remember is that all jerks will eventually show their true colors. You just have to be ready to act on it when it happens. So whether he's asking you to pay for the first three dates while he looks for work or yells at you in front of your friends, it's never too late to spot the signs, make a clean break, and move on with your life.

Q. *"I don't know if I'll ever trust again. I have been hurt really bad, have a history of family problems, am constantly depressed, and am terrified of getting involved with someone. What do I do?"*

A. Here's where I draw the line. I wouldn't even begin to try to solve a lifetime of problems and emotional issues in a neat little paragraph. While some of you may just be in a temporary commitment-averse funk, others of you are dealing with weighty issues that you've probably spent a lifetime trying to unravel. Whether you've gone through the divorce of your parents, lost a caregiver early in life, or been the victim of any form of abuse, there's no quick solution that will solve all your commitment problems overnight. Issues of trust, abandonment anxiety, or prolonged feelings of hopelessness brought on by adverse life circumstances should be your cue to seek out a trusted mental health practitioner who makes you feel comfortable and allows you to open up in a safe setting.

The laws of attraction dictate that emotionally healthy people will be drawn to each other, and that emotionally unhealthy partners will somehow attract each other as well. It's the universe's way of righting itself. That's why it's important to heal yourself, so you can start attracting more stable partners. If you're depressed, suffering from anxiety, or feeling hopeless, your romantic relationships are bound to suffer due to inappropriate reactions and subversive behavior that will undermine your goals. It's only by working through your issues from the past that you'll be able to attract someone who's emotionally together and won't leave you running for the door. Of course, no amount of therapy can help someone who's not ready to confront her own issues. So before you take to the analyst's couch, take a minute to answer these questions.

1. Are you ready to admit that you may be holding on to pent-up feelings of anger, sadness, and regret as a way to shield yourself from further pain?
2. Are you ready to stop letting your past drive your current behaviors?
3. Are you open to the idea that you can change your life by changing your thoughts?
4. Are you ready to forgive the people who have hurt you in the past?
5. Are you ready to take responsibility for your role in current relationships?

THE DOCTOR IS IN

I think relationship trauma has a huge impact on people's ability to commit, especially if the trauma was not healed and put into some context where it made sense. What happens is that you transfer your fears from one relationship to the next. The first thing to do is to address any kind of traumas that are still there, to heal old wounds. A lot of it has to do with childhood trauma. If our earliest relationships with our caregivers are our most important and if our caregivers were negligent or abusive, uninvolved, or uninterested, that makes for a rocky foundation to begin with.

—*Debra Mandel, Ph.D.*

Q. *"I just don't think I'm ready for anything. I've put on lots of weight and have really let myself go. Who would want to be with me in this state?"*

A. Here's a great way to avoid commitment: put on weight, don't take care of your appearance, and then assume that all your relationship problems are due to other people's superficiality. You figure, "Hey, if he was really that special, he wouldn't care what I looked like, right?" WRONG! I don't care how special or down-to-earth the guy is; *everyone* notices appearance. Your image and how you take care of yourself play a huge role in how the world sees you. If you're telling people you don't like yourself or don't care to be admired, you can be sure no one else will.

So what do you do? Well, here's what you *don't* do:

1. **You don't go on a crash diet.** Depriving yourself of food because you feel you're not good enough to eat is just plain wrong. Treat yourself well by consulting with a nutritionist, exercising, and avoiding processed foods.

2. **You don't wait until you lose weight to start acting like you're the bomb.** There are plenty of ways to put your best foot forward without having to shop for a skinnier wardrobe. Buy a red scarf to bring out your highlights, wear your favorite jewelry when shopping for groceries, and get your hair done for absolutely no reason. If you start acting like you matter, eventually you'll believe it.

3. **You don't avoid interacting with others.** Weight gain and not taking care of your looks can be ways to buffer yourself from personal interaction. You'd rather risk being rejected for external qualities than face getting rejected for something internal, such as your personality. That's why you'll have to slowly start finding your way back to the world and learning to deal with all your insecurities. Whether you join an acting class or a book club where you can sit on the sidelines for a little while, make an effort to start mingling, pronto!

THE DOCTOR IS IN

Two of the ways that women might avoid commitment are by gaining weight and not taking care of themselves. I think that can be self-protective. I don't think you have to go to the spa all the time to be in a relationship. But there are times when people don't want to be in a relationship and they gain weight and don't take care of themselves. I think that's more of a reflection of how they feel about themselves on the inside. Because they don't feel good about themselves, they feel they don't deserve to be in a relationship, so they gain weight. I think it's all very connected. —*Allison Moir-Smith, M.A.*

DAMSEL IN DISTRESS RECAP

I hope you Damsels are a little less distressed than when you first started reading this chapter. But just in case, this quick recap should cheer you up.

- No matter how many times you think a guy has wronged you, you're not going to get over your commitment issues by laying all the blame on men.

- Getting stuck in the past is one of the easiest ways to avoid commitment.

- If you're too busy romanticizing or demonizing an old love, there's no way you'll end up in a new relationship.

- While you shouldn't assume all your relationship problems are somehow your fault, it's important that you recognize what role you played.

- Instead of worrying about heartache, laugh boldly in its face and just say, "Bring it on!"

- If you keep telling yourself you don't want a committed relationship, you'll probably start to believe it.

- Focusing on what kind of men you don't want to meet is the surest way to attract the very types you're looking to avoid.

- Boundaries are tricky: if you don't have clear ones outlined in the beginning of a relationship, expect to have them trespassed.

- If you can't think of even one thing you did to contribute to your relationship problems, think harder!

8

The Player

Before anyone misconstrues anything I am about to say, here's where I stand on sex and the single girl:

1. Birth control was invented for a good reason.
2. Women who like sex are neither immoral or slutty (unless you mean that in a nice way).
3. *She* definitely comes first.
4. And my idea of a "return to modesty" runs more along the lines of wearing turtlenecks in winter.

As shocking as it may seem, some women actually enjoy sex without the promise of commitment. With sexual liberation in full swing, shows such as *Sex and the City*, new Viagra-like products being marketed to women, Heidi Fleiss opening a new studfarm that's essentially a brothel for women, and books such as *The Happy Hook-Up* and *The Hookup Handbook* advocating an "anything they can do, we can do better" approach to sex, there's a new breed of commitment-phobe on the loose: the Player.

Commonly known as "man-eaters," Players are always hungry for new sexual experiences, go through one guy after another, and collect notches on their Prada belts like sailors on bar stools. Players and Serial Daters have a lot in common, but instead of just dating a variety of men, Players are bedding them, often bypassing the drinks-and-dinner phase altogether. The Player usually goes after a guy, sleeps with him, and then dismisses him before he's had the chance to prove himself—or even cook breakfast, for that matter. While some women can't seem to separate love and sex, Players are all too slick in this department and can neatly compartmentalize their urges the way most women do their makeup drawers. Many of them are addicted to the highs of bedding a new man every night, and make no apologies for their behavior.

Despite the fact that our society still calls promiscuous women "sluts" and men who do the same thing "lucky," the Player couldn't care less about the old sexual double standard. For all that talk about men and women having different sexual wiring, the Player confounds the neat stereotypes and enjoys getting as much as she does giving. Whether it's short-lived affairs, friends-with-benefits scenarios, or favoring one-night stands over traditional relationships, the Players of the world are so giddy with their new sense of sexual empowerment that the idea of sleeping with one man forever leaves them cold and running for the door.

THE CONFESSIONAL: Renée, 28

Whenever I meet a guy, I don't care if he's cute or just average—I automatically think what it would be like to have sex with him. In fact, it seems that the less compatible we are, the more I want to sleep with him. I don't know if it's just boredom, but after a few hours of listening to him drone on and on about his career, hopes, and dreams, all I want to do is just make out. I don't know, maybe I just have lots of testosterone or whatever, but ever since I was little, all I remember thinking about is boys and sex. Of course, the next morning all I can think about is how to get him out of my apartment quickly.

While no one would begrudge the thoroughly modern Millie a little bit of fun, one has to wonder what she is avoiding. Many Players have difficulties relating to men, and feel that they can better control relationships that are based solely on sex. While it wouldn't be fair to say that all women who profess to love strings-free sex are frauds hiding in Player clothing, it's important to consider whether sex has become their sole outlet for emotional intimacy.

This chapter will broach some of the reasons for the Player's sexual openness, and explore how sex can be used as a barrier to intimacy rather than a path toward it. Most important, it will also help Players come to grips with the driving motivation that leads them to seek out casual sex at the expense of committed relationships.

So whether you're tearing off your clothes before the cork is even out of the wine bottle, hooking up with a friend during your biweekly booty call, or cheating on a spouse or boyfriend, you probably have some unexamined issues concerning the role that sex plays in your commitment-phobia. The question you have to ask yourself is what's really behind your tough, horny-girl bravado. Are you really into sex, or are you using it as a way to shield yourself from commitment?

THE DOCTOR IS IN

Men like women and women like men. I think this is an area where maybe women are not as different from men as most people thought they were. Women can definitely get addicted to new sexual experiences. It comes back to the same thing: any addiction is an escape from fear and pain. And so the women's fear of losing control and abandonment can express as avoidance of that through the constant pursuit of new sexual experiences. There's another factor in here, which is the distrust of men, often stemming from negative early experiences, probably with the father. More and more, I see women who are patterning themselves after the male Don Juan model.

—*Dr. Deborah Anapol*

PLAYER TYPECASTING

If you think all female Players are the same, think again. With so many Don Juanitas running loose, it's hard to fit them all into one category.

1. **The "It's Just Sex" Player.** This Player is all about the game, and enjoys sex for its own sake. To her, hooking up is just another fun way to spend an evening, much like going out for a good meal or a night at the theater.

2. **The Rebound Player.** The Rebounder uses sex as a quick fix for getting over a recent breakup. She subscribes to the philosophy that the fastest way to get over an old guy is to get under a new one.

3. **The Attention-Seeking Player.** Some girls just can't get enough attention. And if they need to have sex to keep a guy's interest, they're prepared to go the extra mile or two.

4. **The CEO Player.** If this Player could schedule a quickie in her corner office in between her afternoon meetings, she would. When it comes to the CEO Player, her fast-paced life dictates her sexual motto: "It's not personal, it's just business."

5. **The Angry Player.** Whether she's been scorned in the game of love or was treated as a sex object one too many times, the Angry Player is all about how "two can play that game." She can have sex without feelings, too—or at least that's what she tells herself.

 ## QUIZ: ARE YOU A PLAYER?

While some of you pretty much have a handle on your Player status, others aren't quite so sure where they fit in. Do a couple of one-night stands count? Does sneaking off for an afternoon quickie with a stranger qualify you? Does having sex with an ex-boyfriend even get you in the Player ballpark? No doubt about it, it's all a bit confusing. Take this quiz to find out what separates the players from the amateurs.

1. **How often do you think about sex?**
   A. Just about every five minutes.
   B. A few times a day.
   C. Once a week or if I'm with someone special.

2. **You're at work and you've just been introduced to a new colleague. He's hot, hot, hot! You imagine:**
   A. The two of you horizontal on your desk.
   B. Cuddling in front of a roaring fire in a remote mountain resort.
   C. Working side by side. I don't hook up with guys I work with.

3. On which date do you think it's okay to sleep with a guy?

    A. If doing shots at a bar counts as a date, one should suffice.

    B. Two or three dates is pretty standard for me.

    C. It usually takes a few months or so for me to feel really comfortable.

4. How many sexual partners have you had?

    A. I've long lost track.

    B. I'm pretty sure it's about _____ (fill in the blank with any number over 10).

    C. I can count my sexual partners on one or two hands.

5. What are your requirements for a love interest?

    A. That he be well endowed and know how to please me in bed.

    B. I want a guy who's attractive and fun. Chemistry is *sooo* important!

    C. You know, the basic stuff—caring, loyal, funny.

6. When do you feel closest to the guy you're seeing?

    A. When I'm helping him dial a cab right after sex.

    B. After a night out with lots of smooching in the corner booth.

    C. When we've shared something intimate with each other during a long talk.

7. You just had a one-night stand with an insignificant other. The next morning you:

    A. Rack your brain to remember his name as you rush him out the door.

    B. Invite him to stay for breakfast and coffee.

    C. Feel a little awkward and embarrassed. You never do this, *really*!

8. You're having Sunday brunch with the girls. When they ask you about last night's date, you:

    A. Tell them all the naughty details and throw in a few salacious bits for entertainment value.

    B. Smile knowingly and tell them you had a very nice time.

    C. Change the subject quickly. You hate to kiss and tell!

9. Your favorite first-date outfit is usually:
   A. A clingy formfitting dress with stiletto heels.
   B. Snug jeans and a shoulder-baring top.
   C. A swingy knee-length skirt and a pretty cardigan.

10. What's hiding in your nightstand drawer?
   A. Condoms and a vibrator.
   B. Lingerie.
   C. Books.

Scoring: To calculate your final score, assign a point value to each answer: 3 for every A, 2 for every B, and 1 for every C. Now add it all up and see where you rank.

23–30 Points: Going Pro

You refute the threadbare notions of proper, ladylike behavior and don't see anything wrong with having a little bit of fun. Okay, in your case, we're talking a lot of fun. While it's great to be liberated and sexually empowered, yours may be a case of too much of a good thing. If you're finding that sex has become your one method of interacting with men, you may be setting yourself up for future problems down the line. After all, as fun as sex can be, relating to people in an open and honest way has its own rewards.

15–22 Points: Player in Training

You've probably made your fair share of letter-to-*Penthouse*-worthy sparks. And while you're definitely a sexually liberated kind of gal, you can't seem to shake the idea that you have to wait until the third date to hop in the sack, often insisting on dinner and a movie to green-light your sexploits. So while you may be more guarded about revealing your inner hussy, that doesn't mean you aren't a Player.

14 or Fewer Points: Amateur-Ville

When it comes to dating, your tastes run more along the lines of soul mates, flowers, long kisses, and plenty of cold showers. You see absolutely no reason to jump in the sack right away, especially if you don't know if the guy is right for you. While no one would accuse you of being a prude, you're definitely an old-fashioned kind of girl who would rather have a nice long conversation that a night of unbridled passion.

TOP PLAYER PROTESTS:
"I'M NOT A PLAYER, I'M JUST . . ."

Look, no one's saying that fooling around isn't a blast, because it is. But if you're constantly on the hunt for booty calls and one-night stands, you may find yourself spiraling into a full-blown case of commitment-phobia. While enjoying casual sex once in a while is okay (and even necessary during those in-between-boyfriends stages), if it's the only way you can interact with men, it may become a barrier in your ability to be intimate. So if you're still unsure whether you're a die-hard Player, see if any of these Player protests sound familiar: "I'm not a player, I'm just . . ."

1. **"I'm Just Very Horny."** If you're always thinking about doing the deed and visualizing every man you meet in his boxers (or less), you may just have a higher libido than others. Whether you're into porn, threesomes, or just your standard garden-variety sex, there's no doubt that sexual desire varies from person to person. Many of you have managed to dispense with the shame that accompanies casual sex, and you figure why be stuck home with the Rabbit if you can have relatively safe, risk-free sex with an actual breathing person?

   But is being horny the real issue here? It may be a good excuse to engage in a myriad of affairs and sexual hijinks, but it won't help you get to the root of the commitment matter. While lustiness definitely plays a large part, people have sex for a variety of reasons, including anger, a need for attention, loneliness, or boredom. After all, if it's really such a simple matter of an abnormally high libido, why does your sex drive plummet as soon as the guy starts talking about grabbing some dinner or going on a proper date? Could it be that horniness is really the mask you use to hide your fear of emotional intimacy and commitment?

THE CONFESSIONAL: Cordelia, 31

The thing is, as soon as I get into a relationship, I stop wanting to have sex as much. It's not as fun when I know exactly how they're going to kiss me and in what position. The excitement of the chase is gone, and knowing he's around all the time makes me want to kind of postpone sex for a few days. A few days become weeks and sometimes even months. It's so strange, 'cause when I'm single, all I can do is think about sex—when I'm going to have it, with whom, and what it's going to be like.

2. **"I'm Just Not Attracted to Men Once I Get to Know Them."** Ever find yourself telling a stranger a secret you have never told anyone before—not to your best friend, sibling, boyfriend, or parents? It's amazing how open and uninhibited we can be with people we've just met.

    Well, the same principle applies to sex. While some women would cringe at the thought of doing it with a total stranger, others find that they are more comfortable and open to having sex with someone they hardly know. In fact, one-night stands and casual encounters allow them to express their hidden desires and fulfill fantasies in a way that they would never dare to in a committed relationship.

    Many of you figure that once you're in a relationship, it's not as easy to take sexual risks and go buck wild. You worry about what the guy will think of you and how you're coming across, and may feel more inhibited in showcasing some of your raunchier moves. It's the same reason some men seek out prostitutes, for fear if they asked their wives or girlfriends to perform whatever unspeakable acts they've thought up, they would be forced to sleep on the couch for the next twenty years.

    If you find yourself more attracted to strangers than people you're emotionally connected to, ask yourself what is so scary about sharing some of your naughty fantasies within the confines of a committed relationship. Are you scared of appearing vulnerable? Do you worry about being judged or rejected? The reason sex gets boring in committed relationships is because most people are too afraid to discuss what it is they want and they don't trust each other to be that open. It just takes getting over some of your personal hang-ups and having the courage to speak openly about your wanton, lusty needs. In fact—and this may be somewhat of a shocker—some women actually think that the more they love someone, the better the sex, since the act becomes more about sharing rather than just going for the big O.

So if you find that you're losing interest in a steady guy and hunger for that exciting anonymous experience, keep in mind that there's absolutely no reason you can't be uninhibited with someone you're committed to. And if all else fails, just blindfold your guy, whisper something dirty in his ear, and fantasize about all the anonymous men you want.

3. **"I'm Not a Player, I'm Just One of the Guys."** If you can guzzle beer, swear like a sailor, pour a mean dirty martini, and play hold-'em poker until the wee hours of the morning, you're probably what's known as a "guy's girl," women who tend to feel more comfortable scrapping it up with the boys than sharing all their intimate secrets with their girlfriends. Being around so many men, it's not uncommon for these types of women to adopt a more "male" attitude toward sex. And that's precisely where things often go awry. Because while some women may think that they have a good idea of what it's like for men to have sex—shutting down their feelings, avoiding intimacy, and being conquest-oriented—most of our views about male sexuality are completely skewed.

Common consensus has it that men can just jump into bed without any worries, hang-ups, or second thoughts, but that just isn't the reality. In fact, while guys will tell their friends one thing in an attempt to seem macho, they usually experience a whole host of other feelings they would never admit to.

Men have plenty of issues in the sex department, including body image ("Is it big enough?"), performance anxiety ("Did I do that right?"), and feeling objectified ("She's just using me, but I like it"). In the end, what guys reveal to their friends about their sex lives during a night of binge drinking is very different from what's really going on beneath the surface, including a whole host of emotional issues you could never even begin to guess at. So while no one's saying that you can't have sex "like one of the guys," at least make sure you know exactly what that means in the first place—because in your effort to beat men at their own game, you may end up losing out on some deeply meaningful interactions.

TOP PLAYER HANG-UPS

Even if you have no hang-ups in the sex department, that doesn't mean you're not hung up in the commitment department. While some of you are perfectly satisfied with your take-no-prisoners persona, many of you are legitimately concerned that sex has become your only way of connecting with men. If you find that you fit into the latter category, check out some of the other pitfalls you may eventually fall into.

1. Too Much Sex

Whether it's your favorite mocha latte, cigarettes, or your iPod, anything can be habit-forming, including sex. No one's saying that you qualify for a clinical diagnosis of sex addiction (not yet, anyway), but you might be more hooked than you think. While I would never begrudge you some fun, it's important that you make an effort to get to know at least a few men you date on a platonic level. As you go on dates, think about how you use sex to avoid dealing with painful emotions, such as loneliness or fear of rejection. Figure out when you're most sexually aroused and what triggers you. Is it alcohol, a feeling that you may actually like the guy, or a need to distract yourself? Of course, getting to know your dates doesn't mean grilling them about all their sexual turn-ons and -offs. That's right—absolutely no talk of sex or even thinking about sex on the first two dates. Think of it as an experiment to see how the other half lives.

In the end, jumping in the sack too soon and too often may numb you to the emotional side of the experience, leading you to objectify men and see them purely as sex objects rather than as human beings. And while you may say, "So what? Men have been doing it for years to women!" ask yourself if your sexual compulsions are motivated by revenge, competition, or anger rather than just good old-fashioned lust.

2. Pseudo-Relationships

Sex and food have a lot in common. Sometimes you want a long, drawn-out meal complete with white tablecloths, fine china, candles, and a sommelier. Other times, you want a fast fix at the drive-through, something that will satisfy you quickly, without any commitment. Much like the latter scenario, the friends-with-benefits scenario can be a very tempting proposition when you're hungry for some drive-through lovin'. After all, who could resist a situation where two people can have all the sex they want without any of the stress of an emotional commitment? It's like eating an entire chocolate cake without consuming any calories.

Friends with benefits are like an old, reliable blanket; they're always around and ready to warm you up. Not only are they nice, sweet, and already your friends, you don't have to feel icky scouring singles bars looking for guys who may or may not be shady. It's all too easy to get caught up in these no-muss, no-fuss situations. After all, who has time for a steady boyfriend when you're juggling school, work, or any of the million other things you're doing? And while it may seem innocent enough at first, once you get used to having these quasi-committed relationships, it's going to be hard to accept a real relationship that actually requires work, energy, and accountability.

THE CONFESSIONAL: Kaley, 26

Now that I'm married, I'm kicking myself for not waiting to see if I could do better—and I'm trying to remember what I was thinking seven months ago when I married this guy. I thought that was it. I thought this guy is great. He absolutely adores me. I love him. I'm very attracted to him. He's the best lover I had. So there are a lot of good things. I used to have booty-call guys that I would call up in different cities depending on which nightclub I went to or which area I was in. If I was going to be in LA for a concert, I would call up the one in LA and say, "What are you doing?" I'm starting to miss the days when I had lovers and I'd give them a call and we'd hang out Friday through Sunday and then we wouldn't see each other for weeks or months. It's just the weekend relationship package deal, where you get the nice romance, the dinner, the little conversation, and the small talk. And Sunday morning after breakfast we both go our separate ways. I miss that. If I wasn't married, that's what I'd be doing. It was nice having the freedom and not having to deal with someone else's emotional things.

3. The "Hot Mama" Syndrome

While it's great to feel sexually uninhibited and alive, some women are so proud of their newfound empowerment that they go overboard and end up emphasizing this one quality to the exclusion of many others. While it may sound perfectly harmless, the "hot mama" syndrome sets in when a woman feels that she has to live up to an overly sexualized persona.

With so much talk about whom you're having sex with, when, where, and in what position, people will start to believe that sex is your full-time preoccupation. After all, your friends have probably grown to rely on you to come through with new stories of sexcapades, to the point where you now feel that you would be letting them and yourself down if you don't at least provide a few salacious tidbits.

But here's the deal: if you're always talking about sex and boasting about your conquests, you'll get trapped into acting that way even when you're tired of fooling around and are ready to get more serious. Once you've reduced your identity to its sexual core, it will get harder and harder to break out of the mold, since everyone will expect you to act in sexually suggestive ways. So while you may indeed be a sexy, hot, and liberated mama, make sure you don't place undue emphasis on this one personality trait at the expense of all the other qualities that make you, well, *you!*

GET OVER IT: SUREFIRE STRATEGIES

At first, casual sex may seem like a fun female prerogative—and for a while, it can be! But if you find that your wanton sexual ways are becoming a way of life, consider the impact it can have on your ability to open up to another person. While no one's saying you should join a nunnery or commit yourself to a life of celibacy, there are ways to curb your behavior and establish intimacy, all without sacrificing sexual fulfillment. Still not convinced? Check out some of these strategies.

> **Q.** *"I think casual sex is pretty damn intimate. I think how we act in the bedroom reveals a lot about who we are. Why do you think it's a sign I have commitment-phobia?"*

A. I completely understand. Why have an honest-to-goodness conversation about anything serious when a back rub feels so much better? While sex can definitely be an intimate act with the right person in the right relationship, premature or casual sex with someone you hardly know is one good way to ensure you never actually find out anything of value about them. Not that you can't move from a casual sex relationship to a deeply intimate one, but if you're not careful, sex can quickly become a crutch to help you avoid dealing with anything remotely touchy-feely, real, or sentimental.

And I agree, sex *can* and often does reveal a lot about who we are. It reveals our attitude toward power, how we feel about ourselves, and a whole slew of other things that have nothing to do with the sexual act per se. But that's only in relationships based on trust and understanding. Because while you may find out something about your sexy stranger's quirks and eccentricities, it's doubtful he'll be comfortable enough to reveal anything truly personal. Not only will you establish a relationship that's based solely on sex, it will be very hard to move past that phase, since both of you will become accustomed to expressing yourself solely through sex. In fact, some couples end up having sex all the time to compensate for the lack of emotional intimacy in their relationship.

So if you're trying to find out more about a stranger by having sex with him, you may want to try another tactic. A better way may be to try to get out of your comfort zone. Instead of jumping into bed before you even find out his last name, take a risk, ask some probing questions, and settle in for a good talk (clothing *not* optional).

Q. "So if I'm in between relationships, are you saying I should abstain from sex? That would be pretty hard!"

A. I firmly believe that a girl's got to do what a girl's got to do. There's something about being fresh out of a relationship that makes you want to go forth, explore, and conquer. After having consistent sex for months or years with a steady boyfriend, not knowing where your next fix is coming from can send even the most even-keeled vixen into a tizzy of sexual starvation. So telling you to abstain would be like telling a male construction worker not to whistle at passing women.

While you may not want to forsake sex altogether after a breakup, do try to limit your sexual interaction to one shag buddy. I know, I said friends with benefits was a bad idea, but that's only for women who make it a way of life. For you, designating one person as your sex partner may just be your saving grace. Once your sexual needs are fulfilled, you won't try to bed every single guy who crosses your path, and you can spend some time getting to know each one on a deeper level.

Another helpful strategy would be to give yourself a hooking-up deadline—somewhere in the three-to-four-month range. During that time, you can engage in all the casual sex you want (much like an all-you-can-screw buffet), provided, of course, that you're being safe. Once that time is up, you can curtail your postbreak sex romp and start focusing on building real relationships, whether it's with yourself, your friends and family, or a possible new admirer. So while many of you will go through a trial Player period after a breakup (a.k.a. "binge screwing"), don't let it become a habit long after you've nursed your wounds and sowed your oats.

THE CONFESSIONAL: Alyssa, 23

I detach most of my feelings when I'm having sex with someone. I had sex with this guy about three weeks ago. I met him online, but he was a friend of a friend. So he came and picked me up, and we went on a date. Things were good. He said, "I really want to hang out this weekend. I like you," blah, blah, blah. He lived in Connecticut. I knew Connecticut was too far and I wasn't really into him, but I felt like he might like me. I was like, "Uh-oh, what am I going to do?" So I figured if I had sex with him we would probably never talk again.

Q. "Just because I have a lot of sex doesn't mean I don't have feelings or that I'm emotionally shut down. What's up with that?"

A. Trial and error has taught us that there's no use falling in love with every guy we sleep with. With so much more of our time spent single, it's understandable in this day and age that women would become more adept at separating sex from love. But while emotional detachment may help us have no-strings-attached sex, it can also lead to repressing many healthy feelings of intimacy that will be hard to excavate once we've found someone we could actually care about. All those times when you forced yourself not to care or even bother thinking about the other person may become a hard habit to break.

No matter how you slice it, being a Player and going on sex sprees may make you feel liberated, but it will eventually take a significant emotional toll. You may become good at separating love and sex, but there is such a thing as being too good at controlling your feelings. Not only that, the behavior can also be a passive way of rejecting many nice guys, since having premature sex is a great way to eliminate any chance of them ever calling you again. You figure, "Why bother rejecting him when I can have sex with him on the first date?"

In the end, your feelings cannot just be turned on and off like hot water. If you don't practice being vulnerable and showing how you feel, your emotional faucets are bound to get rusty. So what's the solution? Well, it's not going to happen overnight. You'll need to practice revealing sides of your personality that don't revolve around sex. Whether you're hanging with friends or out on a first date, try to think about how you're presenting yourself, and ask yourself why you feel more comfortable talking about sex than all those hopes and dreams that don't involve joining the mile-high club. Once you practice opening up, start focusing on serious issues that affect you, and discover other outlets for fulfilling yourself emotionally, the idea of having sex with every guy you meet may just suddenly lose its allure.

THE PLAYER INSTANT RECAP

If you're worried that this is the end of the Player line, rest assured you can still have a good time without reverting to your old ways. Of course, change is always a scary proposition, and you might feel uncomfortable trying to relate to men on a nonsexual level, at least at first. So whenever you need a reason to avoid jumping in the sack, turn to this page for a quickie refresher course.

- If you're not careful, sex can quickly become a crutch to help you avoid dealing with real emotions.

- While enjoying casual sex once in a while is okay (and even necessary during those in-between-boyfriends stages), if it's the only way you can interact with men, it may become a barrier in your ability to be intimate.

- It's okay to want to have sex "like one of the guys"—putting feelings on hold, shunning intimacy, and being conquest-oriented—but don't forget that your view of male sexuality may be completely skewed.

- Premature or casual sex with someone you hardly know is one good way to ensure you never actually find out anything about him.

- If you're always talking about sex and boasting about your conquests, you'll get trapped into acting that way even when you're tired of fooling around.

- If you get used to the ease and comfort of friends-with-benefits relationships, it's going to be that much harder to engage in real relationships that actually require work, energy, and commitment.

- Having sex too often can lead you to objectify men and see them purely as sex objects rather than human beings.

- Feelings cannot just be turned on and off like hot water. If you don't practice being vulnerable and showing how you feel, your emotional faucets are bound to get rusty.

9

The Long-Distance Runner

LISA
I'm sure she'll call. Six years is a
long time. You don't just break it off
cleanly after six years.

MIKE
I know, but she did. She's with someone
else now. . . .

LISA
It's a rebound.

MIKE
We were a rebound, and we lasted six
years.

LISA
Yeah, but how long was the relationship
she was rebounding *from*?

MIKE
Six years.

—*Swingers*, 1996

elationship junkies, serial monogamists, perpetual couplers—whatever you call them, Long-Distance Runners are some of the most complicated commitment-phobes around. While Serial Daters are hooked on the romance part—flowers, lust, first kisses—Long-Distance Runners are addicted to relationships, often jumping from one long-term union to another.

What's interesting about this group is that nothing about the Runner's outward behavior reflects her fear of commitment. You would never know that she was a commitment-phobe just by looking at her. Never one to be accused of flightiness or irresponsible behavior, she wears her dependability like a badge and has usually been involved in a series of long relationships that have failed to go anywhere. This is the girl who stayed with her high school sweetheart for many years and then went on to stay with her college sweetheart for many years. She may have been married, been engaged several times, lived with someone for years, or just gotten involved in one marathon union after another. And yet she still finds herself unable to maintain an emotional connection that stands the test of time. While their relationship patterns may vary, all Runners have one thing in common—they're terrified of making a lasting commitment.

Unlike the Serial Dater who tends to move from one brief relationship to the next, Long-Distance Runners always find themselves in long-term relationships and appear as if they're in it for the long haul. And while both Serial Daters and Long-Distance Runners are equally scared of making a commitment, Runners are less likely to see themselves as commitment-phobic due to the length of the unions they engage in.

THE CONFESSIONAL: Penelope, 39

I'd been in many long-term relationships. In my twenties I was married for five years. Then immediately I went into another five-year relationship. I've spent 80 percent of the time not wanting to be in those relationships and acted like a single person. I kept it a secret that I was married. I didn't have affairs, but I was very resentful of being married and I was very resentful of being in a long-term relationship. Whenever a relationship does start, after that first couple of months of magic and the power struggle starts coming in, I don't like it. I get very antsy.

When it comes to relationships, Long-Distance Runners can't survive without one for very long. They just loved to be loved, and when they don't have someone at their side, they quickly jump into another relationship that goes on and on without any clear goal of permanent commitment in sight. They enjoy all the benefits that come with relationships—support, security, affection—but don't like the icky commitment part of it. Basically, they want to eat their cake and have it, too: all the security of a committed union with none of the risky emotional intimacy that usually goes along with it. They may even agree to marry and stay long enough to let the ink dry on the marriage certificate, but when it comes down to actually giving the relationship their all, these runaway commitment-phobes are nowhere to be found.

Despite the fact that they engage in marathon unions, Long-Distance Runners tend to avoid talking about marriage or discussing the future. In fact, they'll often pick a man with a fundamental incompatibility—age, religion, or geographic location—which they can point to as the deciding breakup factor when the relationship ends. Call it a built-in escape hatch when things get too scary. Whether it's signing a lease, buying new furniture, or even talking about the future, every time the commitment level looks like it's escalating, Long-Distance Runners will do anything in their power to steer things off course, including picking fights, criticizing, or bolting without warning.

THE CONFESSIONAL: Stacy, 34

A few years ago, I had been with someone for almost eight years and we started talking about getting married. That's when I started panicking and I decided to move out of state. I just started thinking, "Oh my God, what if I miss something?" I guess it's a pattern with me. As soon as things get too serious, I run. The breakup was awful. It was probably on my top five list of the worst things you can go through. He was definitely someone I could see myself being with long-term. He could have been the right person, but I did leave him, which makes me wonder about myself.

Elina Furman

It may seem counterintuitive to say that some of the biggest commitment panickers are people who can't stand to be alone. But that's the truth. Many of you are as scared of being alone as you are of committing. While many of you think that your marathon relationship history proves you have zero issues with commitment, consider that engaging in long-term unions that never work out is an all-too-common commitment-phobic pattern. After all, length is not an indicator of depth. Just because you're in a long relationship doesn't mean that the level of intimacy and commitment is strong; you may just be hiding out from the prospect of meeting someone you are truly compatible with on a grander scale. So if you think you fit this description and are tired of engaging in a string of long-term but dead-end relationships that never seem to go anywhere, this chapter is for you.

THE DOCTOR IS IN

Our culture socializes us to think that we should be in relationships, which is what happens with serial monogamists. These people may be the most commitment-phobic because they go from long-term relationship to long-term relationship. The question is, how deeply intimate are they with their partners? Are they truly partners and sharing their lives and sharing who they are? Or are they too scared to do that?

—*Allison Moir-Smith, M.A.*

QUIZ: ARE YOU A LONG-DISTANCE RUNNER?

You may not be as bad as J. Lo in the serial monogamy department, but if you keep jumping from one long relationship to another and bolt whenever anything gets too serious, you may just be a Long-Distance Runner. Here's one foolproof way to find out once and for all.

1. **What was the longest time you ever spent single?**
   A. A month tops.
   B. Six months to a year.
   C. Two or more years.

2. **When you see a single girl sitting at a table of couples, you think:**
   A. Oh, poor dear, she must be miserable and dying to be in a relationship.
   B That's odd—maybe she's visiting from out of town.
   C. It's cool to see someone so unfazed by the need to be in a couple.

3. **Finish this sentence: "Being in an okay relationship is better than . . ."**
   A. Being alone.
   B. Dating. I hate being "out there."
   C. Got me. Every relationship is different.

4. **How comfortable are you having dinner alone at a crowded restaurant?**
   A. I would be mortified!
   B. Not very. I'd feel like everyone was judging me.
   C. I'm okay as long as I have some reading material.

5. **When you find yourself bored in a long-term relationship, what do you usually do?**
   A. Think about leaving or hook up with someone new.
   B. Get annoyed with my guy for being such a snooze ball.
   C. Come up with fun new things for us to do.

6. **What's your favorite part of being in a relationship?**
   A. I don't have to tell people I'm single.
   B. I don't have to worry about holidays or when I need a date to a wedding.
   C. Sharing, caring, and baring. It's all about opening myself up emotionally to someone.

7. What was your last breakup like?

A. We were dating for two years, and then I met someone new and broke off with the old guy.

B. The breakup was hard on me, but I met someone great just a few months later.

C. It was partly mutual and I am taking some time off from dating just to get over the whole thing.

8. Do you often think and talk about marriage when you're in a relationship?

A. I try not to, especially if things are going well.

B. Sometimes, but I tend to avoid it.

C. Yes. I would never get involved in a relationship that didn't have a future.

9. How do you feel about compromise in a relationship?

A. It's okay, so long as he's doing most of it.

B. I tend to give in a lot in the early stages but then get frustrated after a while.

C. Both people need to compromise to have a healthy relationship.

10. Your friends invite you for a girls' night out. What's your main goal?

A. To find a great guy who's relationship material.

B. To flirt and have fun.

C. To bond with the girls.

Scoring: To calculate your final score, assign a point value to each answer: 3 for every A, 2 for every B, and 1 for every C. Then add it all up to see how you score.

23–30 Points: Going, Going, Gone!

It's fair to say the single life is not for you. When it comes to relationships, you can't live without them. Well, not for long anyway. Many times, an old liaison hasn't even had a postmortem exam before you get involved with someone new. Since you probably haven't given yourself enough time to be on your own, it's only natural that you're having a hard time committing.

15–22 Points: Runner in Training

You have all the traits of the Long-Distance Runner but none of the obsessive need to be coupled at any cost. While you prefer relationships to casual trysts, you're still working on learning how to balance your own needs with those of a partner. Of course, you do tend to stay in relationships long after their expiration date. So if you find yourself planning your exit for months on end or waiting for some new guy to come along and save you, you may need to take a good long look at what's driving you to get involved in these marathon unions in the first place.

14 or Fewer Points: Runner-Up

While you would never pooh-pooh the ties that bind, you're certainly not a slave to them, either. You know that committing to someone before you've had ample time to be on your own isn't necessarily the best idea. Solo or partnered, you have a balanced view of the compromises and benefits that go along with both scenarios.

LONG-DISTANCE RUNNER PROTESTS: "I'M NOT A RUNNER, I JUST . . ."

Many of you long-distance runners have no idea that you're commitment-phobic. After all, how could you be if you're always in relationships? Problem is, as much as you enjoy toying with the idea of making a commitment, you can never quite go through with it, and instead sabotage promising relationships just as they reach the moment of truth. Protest all you want, but if your objections sound anything like these, you may in fact be a Long-Distance Runner with a questionable commitment track record.

THE CONFESSIONAL: Andrea, 30

As soon as my boyfriend started mentioning getting married someday, I started getting weird. I told him I didn't believe in living together before marriage only because I didn't want to move in together at all. I immediately started thinking about getting a different job in another

place, and made him feel like he was holding me back by not wanting me to go. I even started giving him these guilt trips about not being able to support a family. I told him he had to get his act together before getting serious with me. Which was bull. Really, I just wanted him to get fed up and back off. Eventually, after a couple of months of pressure from him for me to commit to at least thinking about committing, I did take a job—in another country! I moved from England to Connecticut and told him to get over me and move on. I told him that I needed to go out into the world on my own to develop as a person and that we weren't ready to commit to each other. And then I moved away. He was really torn up, but I kind of dissociated from it and really didn't feel too bad. I also got married once, at the age of nineteen, after knowing the guy for a few months. Of course, the marriage lasted about three months before I moved out, mostly because I couldn't imagine never dating again. How horrible is that? And I told him it was because he drank too much.

1. **"I Just Get Bored After a While."** The beginning of a relationship is always an exciting time. You spend all your hours thinking about him, waiting for him to call, and wondering if he truly likes you. But as time goes on and you settle into a comfy groove, you can't help feeling restless in the relationship. For some of you, it may happen after a year. For others, it can strike at the three-year mark. But rest assured, there will always come a time when you get bored or uninspired with yourself, your partner, and the relationship in general.

Whether he's pushing you for a commitment or just happy to share a mutual affection for an indefinite amount of time, at some point you will look at him and wonder, "Is that all there is?" And that's when the trouble starts. Slowly you start focusing on his flaws, dissecting everything he says, and gradually you become more and more dissatisfied. Seemingly overnight and with no warning, "the one" has suddenly become "almost the one."

In most relationships, the going will eventually get tougher. It's not that the guy is not right for you as much as the fact that you've probably grown tired and bored of the situation. It's all too easy to make a hasty exit, thinking that the lack of fire, passion, and excitement is a sign that the relationship isn't working. And without a commitment in place, you won't be as motivated to work out your problems. Of course, boredom is not the issue in itself. It's just a sign that your relationship has stalled and requires more of an emotional investment. In fact, boredom is often the excuse we use to avoid facing our fears of emotional intimacy and taking the relationship to the next level. And while your union may in fact need work and a little spicing up, boredom should be a sign to roll up your sleeves and get cracking, not a sign to abandon ship altogether.

2. **"I'm Just Not Ready."** All the time in the world is not going to make someone ready to commit. If you find that you're still not convinced whether or not you want to be with this person after three years of dating or living together, you should realize that nothing is going to happen that will suddenly change your mind. There will be no lightning bolts, no epiphanies, no signs from above. Either you have to commit yourself wholeheartedly to the union, decide to stay for the sake of convenience, or leave the relationship altogether.

While it may appear as if you're fully invested in the relationship because you're monogamous, living together, or have been dating for many years, that may not be the case. It may mean that you're just committed to having this person by your side for the time being. After all, passing time together and committing to each other are hardly the same thing. At some point, you have to stop collecting dating data and analyzing the relationship. At some point, you just have to make a decision, right or wrong. If you don't, it's all too easy to get caught up in a cycle of emotional paralysis and stagnation, praying for something to happen but being unable to change anything.

THE CONFESSIONAL: Olivia, 33

I was involved with somebody for four and a half years who actually proposed marriage to me after two years of dating. I actually said maybe to the proposal because I wasn't sure if I was ready to get married in general or married to him specifically, and continued to be in the relationship for another two years before breaking it off. For me, it's just a question of not recognizing soon enough that somebody is not right for me when I am in a relationship. So I probably wait too long before making a decision that this is not the right person rather than saying this isn't working out. In the past, I've been in long relationships with people where I knew it wasn't going anywhere. I think now I am more mature and I can recognize it and put an end to it before too much time passes.

3. **"I Just Always End Up in Relationships."** See if you recognize this scenario. You're involved in a long relationship and finally decide that you need to spend some time alone. You break up, move out, and are resolute about wanting your own space. A few weeks or a couple of months go by, and you find yourself lonely, distressed, and hungry for affection, so much so that when you meet someone who seems relationship-worthy, you jump into it with abandon, forgetting all about your pledge to live solo.

If you're always going from one liaison to another and have never spent any amount of time getting to know yourself, you may not be ready to make a permanent commitment. After all, how could you commit to another person if you've never actually made a commitment to *yourself*? Despite the fact that relationships offer a lot of room for personal growth and teach us basic relating skills (like how not to hog the blanket and share bathroom counter space), they don't always provide ample room for self-exploration.

It's important to realize that relationships don't just happen to you. While it can be pretty flattering to be pursued, that doesn't mean you have to get involved with everyone who so much as looks in your direction. Realize that sometimes you choose to be in relationships because they help you feel safe, secure, and in denial about your hidden commitment issues.

Commitment Time Bombs

How many times have you gotten involved with someone with a basic incompatibility, saying, "If we really love each other, it shouldn't matter"? Or "If our relationship is right, things will just work out"? And while some differences may indeed be workable, others are like relationship time bombs just waiting to explode.

Constantly choosing relationships with built-in problems is a way to act out your commitment-phobic behavior patterns. The issue may stay dormant for many years, but at some point it will erupt. You know the expiration date will arrive eventually, which is why you're choosing that person in the first place, since you can point to that issue as the final straw. So while these basic incompatibilities are not absolute deal breakers, they may provide you with a convenient out once you're ready to move on.

THE CONFESSIONAL: Rachel, 34

I'm not particularly religious, but being Jewish is a huge part of who I am. I went to Hebrew school, always wanted to raise my kids Jewish, the works. For me, it's more a cultural thing than anything. So it was weird that every guy I ever dated in high school, college, and throughout my twenties wasn't Jewish. And it's not like I didn't have options—most of the people I was around were Jewish. I even spent five years dating someone who was a bit anti-Semitic, though I pretty much blocked it out. I used to complain that I was never attracted to Jewish guys, but lately I've been thinking that my choices have more to do with my fear of commitment than anything else. After every breakup, I could honestly say I was pretty relieved, since I didn't see it going anywhere because of the religion thing. Maybe it's because I'm getting older, but now I'm very careful about starting relationships with guys who aren't Jewish.

Religious and Cultural Differences. While it's not fair to say that people of different faiths or from different cultural backgrounds can't have a solid committed relationship, it does present some challenges, especially if you're very religious to begin with. In that case, picking people who are not in your cultural or religious dating pool may just be your way of acting out your fear of commitment. Ask yourself: "Is dating someone with the same values important to me? Do I see myself committing to someone who doesn't share my religious beliefs?" If you answered no, then go ahead and be the United Nations of love. But if you do put a high premium on finding someone who shares your beliefs, think twice before launching yourself into a new dating adventure with someone who doesn't fit the bill.

THE CONFESSIONAL: Helena, 28

My last breakup, with a younger guy, was devastating to me. I don't know why I didn't see that we wouldn't work out. Some friends of mine later told me that they knew it wouldn't last. And since girls mature faster than guys, they knew from the start that he was immature and that there was no future in our relationship. I either failed to see that or knew it and just didn't want to accept that. I guess I subconsciously go for the guys that I know it won't work out with or who won't settle down anytime soon.

The Age Gap. It may be all the rage now, but older women dating younger men and vice versa is not necessarily the nirvana it's cracked up to be. And while Demi and Ashton may be proving that age differences don't really matter, constantly dating people who are much older or younger than you may be your not-so-subtle way of saying you're not ready for a commitment, at least not yet. If you see a pattern where you're constantly in relationships with a serious age gap, it may be your own passive-aggressive way of dealing with your commitment fears. Of course, there are many happy December-May hook-ups. But as with any relationship, it helps to figure out if you're on the same page in terms of life goals before tossing all caution to the wind.

So Far, So Good. During my twenties, I spent the majority of time involved in a long-distance relationship. Now, don't get me wrong—at the time, I wouldn't have had it any other way. In fact, it was much like having a virtual boyfriend. I could call him up when I wanted to, and turn him off just as quickly. Not only did I have someone to listen to me for hours on the phone (and the promise of sex every month), I also had all the freedom I needed to concentrate on my career and hang out with my friends and family. Honestly, if I'd been single and dating at that time, I doubt I would have been as productive.

But as much as I denied it back then, long-distance relationships can be extremely deceptive. Since you never spend too much time together, it's all too easy to think the relationship is much better than it is or that the two of you are more compatible than you actually are. Long-distance arrangements provide all the romance and stability of a relationship with none of the work, which is why they're extremely easy to get hooked on.

In the end, it's very hard to get to know someone when you're thousands of miles apart, and it's all too tempting to romanticize the whole situation. Weekends together may be filled with passionate encounters and a full itinerary of cool activities, but it's hardly an accurate gauge of what the relationship will be like once you're living in the same zip code. So if you find yourself making passes at every guy who's just passing through, take it as a clear sign that you may have some serious unresolved commitment issues.

THE CONFESSIONAL: Jeri, 46

I was dating a guy who lived in Arizona. We made frequent trips to see each other. As time went by, he started talking about moving here to Chicago. It would almost give me a sick feeling, but I would brush it off. The next time he came to visit he scheduled interviews in Chicago without telling me, and as soon as I found out I became cold to him the

Elina Furman

TOP LONG-DISTANCE RUNNER HANG-UPS

If you're constantly getting stuck in dead-end relationships for far longer than you should be, you may need to get clear on your motives. While you may pride yourself on going the distance, just because you've spent a lot of time with your guy doesn't mean you're capable of making a commitment to him. Check out the most common Long-Distance Runner hang-ups.

1. If It Ain't Broke . . .

We all know women who have been planning their weddings since birth. They've picked out their wedding color scheme, their dream bridal dress, and the typeface on their invites long before they've even met anyone commitment-worthy. And then there are women who are the exact opposite, those of you who can't stomach wedding talk of any kind. The thought of all that white everywhere, poofy bridesmaid dresses, nonstop photo ops, and till-death-do-you-part business just scares you silly.

It should come as no surprise, then, that Long-Distance Runners tend to avoid any conversation that may bring about change or upset the status quo. It may not even be that you're scared of committing to your man, but more that you're afraid of how a major change will impact your life.

If you're not comfortable talking about marriage and commitment issues after several years of dating, do yourself and your partner a favor and figure out what you're so scared of. It's all well and good to want to stay in your safe and sheltered cocoon, but committed relationships aren't about being safe. In fact, if they're worth anything at all, they'll require us to challenge ourselves, our partners, and our fears of emotional intimacy and commitment. While talking about these subjects is extremely scary, it's important to practice getting comfortable with the idea. So if you're constantly saying "Check, please" as soon as your boyfriends start to talk about the future, don't turn away from your anxiety. Face it and deal with it head-on.

THE CONFESSIONAL: Janet, 27

When conversations about marriage come up something physical happens to me. My throat starts to close up and I start to sweat. I mean, I physically can't even say the word marriage. I can talk about other people's marriages. That's no problem. My friends are getting married, and I'm very happy for them. But when it comes to me and someone starts talking about commitment to me specifically, it really freaks me out.

2. Insta-Fidelity

You meet, you make out, you move in. While one in ten relationships that follow this sequence may actually work out (and make for fantastic dating urban legends), many more will crash and burn. Whether you're just coming out of a breakup or are still putting the finishing touches on your last liaison, you probably don't wait too long to take up with someone new. It could be that you have a hard time saying no to someone or that you just need the validation of being partnered. Whatever it is, you're always finding yourself in a relationship before you even go on a third date.

One of the biggest mistakes Long-Distance Runners make is committing prematurely. They want a relationship so badly that they never really take the time to figure out if the person is right for them. Then, once they're in the relationship, all they can do is think about how wrong the person is, cursing the day they ever met, and biding their time until they can finally get out.

Elina Furman

The best thing you can do is not allow yourself to be pressured into a premature commitment. After all, unless you feel your decision to get involved was based on things like mutual values and respect (not your fear of being alone), you will never be able to fully commit to the relationship no matter how great the guy turns out to be.

THE DOCTOR IS IN

I think when you fall in love too quickly, it's a sign of not being connected to yourself. It's not to say you should be super-careful and vigilant in expecting to be hurt. But when you fall in love too quickly you are not taking into account the other partner. How is he responding to this reaction or this comment or this feeling? Is the relationship being allowed to grow organically or are you forcing it to go somewhere too quickly before it's time? If you do that repeatedly, you really need to look at it. It's okay to yearn and long for a relationship, but it's also a way to sabotage it.

—*Allison Moir-Smith, M.A.*

3. One Foot Out the Door

Keeping one foot out the door may be a person's way of saying, "I love you, I enjoy having you in my life, but I'm scared of committing to you." You may be completely right for each other, but something is stopping you from putting all your effort into the relationship.

Many Long-Distance Runners share a common superstition. You fear that if you admit that you want something—really, really want it—you will somehow end up disappointed. So you end up not really investing yourself in a relationship, fearing that if you do, it will have less of a chance of working out. Seems kind of crazy and irrational, yet many of us share this mind-set.

Of course, having one foot out the door is a way to ensure that the relationship will never work out. Because it makes two people wary and distrustful of each other, this behavior only creates the very reality that you fear. After all, no matter how much you think you're giving, your partner probably notices that you're not investing yourself completely. The question is, would you want to be with someone who's only 50 percent devoted to you? Probably not.

GET OVER IT: SUREFIRE STRATEGIES

There's no doubt that Long-Distance Runners are a complicated lot. While some women can't seem to find a relationship to save their lives, you can't seem to avoid them. Since you're always in a twosome, no one (except your ex-boyfriends) would ever dare accuse you of being commitment-phobic.

Of course, all of this must be very confusing for you. Many of you are desperate to figure out why you're always getting involved in long relationships that never seem to go anywhere. So if you're tired of all the breakups and headaches and are wondering how you'll ever find the motivation to stay the course, check out these strategies that just might do the trick.

> **Q.** *"Maybe I'm being dense, but I still don't get it. How can someone who's always in a relationship be a commitment-phobe?"*

A. Think of it like this: just because you're a shopaholic, it doesn't mean you have good fashion sense. Or just because you like cracking jokes, it doesn't mean you're funny. The same logic applies here. You may enjoy being in relationships, but it doesn't necessarily mean you're good at commitment. Some of you may be hiding behind long-term relationships or even cohabitation arrangements so you can have a relationship without a binding commitment. The key is to figure out if you're pursuing relationships to fill some void in your life. Here are some questions to help you find out:

1. Do you feel empty without a partner in your life?
2. Do you ever feel like a loser for not being part of a couple?

3. Does the idea of being alone fill you with dread?
4. Does being part of a couple make you feel more "normal" and validated?

If you answered yes to any of these questions, you might really want to be in a relationship, but you're certainly not ready to make a commitment. While your obsession with being part of a twosome may be strong, you don't have to fall prey to it.

Think about why you believe that being in a relationship will make you happy. Are you worried that you're not special, pretty, or wonderful when going solo? Do you think women who don't have a partner are somehow judged as less desirable than women who do? If that's why you've been staying in the relationship, consider that you may have to readjust your thinking. After all, no matter how wonderful it feels, a relationship doesn't prove that you're special, witty, or lovely. You don't need to be part of a couple to feel good about yourself. In fact, you might want to try finding other, more substantial ways of boosting your self-esteem, and save the commitment for later when you're a little more sure of who you are.

THE CONFESSIONAL: Carina, 36

This is the first time in at least fifteen years that I have not dated or been in a relationship. It's been extremely hard for me. When I was married, I had no time alone. Then there was an overlap with the last relationship. Even after the last relationship I started dating again right away because I just couldn't deal. So I've been dating off and on forever. It's something that I've finally admitted to myself—that I have commitment issues. It's been one month and it's the longest I've gone on with no distractions and no dating. It's been really, really hard. I've had to really take a look at myself and my life and figure out who I am and construct my identity. I had to look in the mirror without having that relationship serve as my mirror, and learn how to accept myself.

> It's made me take a hard look at myself and my life. Because of the relationships I leaned very heavily on the guy to entertain me and to create a life for me. Now I have to learn to do that for myself.

Q. *"I've left a lot of guys in my day, but I'm convinced they weren't right for me. So how do I know when the guy is not a good fit and when I'm bolting because of my fear of commitment?"*

A. Excellent question! If you don't know if your unhappiness in a relationship has to do with yourself, your partner, or the relationship in general, you're in good company. It can be a very tough matter to sort through. Some Long-Distance Runners will pick people who are truly incompatible or have a fatal flaw, so they always have a valid excuse when ending the relationship. Others will get involved with people who are basically compatible but end up sabotaging the relationship through nit-picking, over-analyzing, and premature evacuation. The key is to figure out which category you fall into.

Fatally Flawed

- You tend to date people who don't share your cultural or religious values.
- You tend to date people with a significant age difference.
- You tend to date people your friends and parents don't approve of.
- You tend to date people who live far away from you.
- You tend to date people with different life goals.

Saboteurs

- You tend to get bored in relationships.
- You tend to criticize your partner for being messy or forgetful.

- You tend to pick fights over minor things.
- You tend to lose interest in sex after a while.
- You tend to blame your boyfriends for your bad moods.

If you fit the first profile, it could very well be that some of your partners may not have been right for you. But that doesn't mean you're off the hook, since choosing them implies that you probably weren't ready to commit in the first place. For the saboteurs out there, it's likely that your commitment anxiety has led you to dismiss one or two good guys that you would have been compatible with. And while some of these men may not have been "the one," it probably has more to do with your attitude toward commitment than with any of your partners per se.

THE CONFESSIONAL: Deidre, 43

I've always had a bit of a problem being alone. I spent most of my twenties in two serious relationships, and then I had another six-year relationship in my early thirties. All the breakups, whether initiated by me or the guy, were extremely painful. I really didn't want to keep going through one painful experience after another. But in my last relationship, I started getting restless and fantasized about leaving every day. I was terrified of having another relationship breakup, and started doing some serious soul-searching. One morning I would wake up and be committed, and the next day I would plot my escape. So finally, I decided that I couldn't go on living with all this uncertainty. I really needed some answers, because at this point I was a complete wreck. I ultimately decided to give myself three months in the relationship with the stipulation that I would be 100 percent committed and try very hard to make it work. I figured I would have nothing to lose, and if things didn't improve between us, then it wouldn't be from my lack of trying. Ultimately, the change in my attitude made a huge difference. We started talking more, going out—it really felt like our relationship improved to some extent. I'm really glad I decided to work things out.

Q. *"You describe me to a T. So how do I get over it? I'm sick of going from one long relationship to another."*

Rest assured, there's definitely a cure. But realize that breaking a lifetime habit will take some serious work. While some people find that being single can be addictive, and they have a hard time merging with someone new, your challenge is to break the cycle of half-assed relationships that you really have no intention of seeing through. Of course, you probably feel scared about being on your own or changing the level of commitment in your current relationship. That's only natural. But if you let your fear of being alone or deepening your emotional bond stop you from making a move, you may just continue to coast along indefinitely.

1. **Work It.** If you've decided to stay in your relationship, rest assured that things will not improve on their own. You've spent a lot of time overanalyzing and vacillating, which has probably created some negativity in the relationship. In order to revive your bond, you'll need to suspend judgment, criticism, restlessness, and boredom—at least for a few months. Think of it as an experiment. Every time you feel commitment panic setting in, recommit yourself to your partner and think of ways to improve the relationship rather than trying to come up with ways to get out. Once you channel your energy in a positive way, you'll finally know whether it's your commitment-phobia that's spoiling things between the two of you or an inherent incompatibility. The first would mean that there's hope for you as a couple, while the latter will mean that you'll have to face your fears of being alone and move on when the time is right. One way or another, you'll finally have your answer.

2. **Pause It.** If you're just coming out of a long relationship, it's all too easy to want to jump into something new. Unfortunately, what can start out as an innocent distraction or a self-esteem boost can end up becoming another drawn-out re-

lationship that prevents you from doing any real inner work, or at the very worst a short-lived rebound relationship in which you end up hurting the other person. Since most of you Long-Distance Runners have a way of attracting partners when you least expect it, avoid dating for a few months and take time out to evaluate what you want to do differently the next time around.

3. **Rewind.** Once you've paused, reserve some time to ponder the role that relationships have played in your life. Despite the fact that many of you have had good relationships in the past, there's obviously something preventing you from making a commitment. So ask yourself: "What are the patterns in my relationships? Why do I think so many of them have not worked out? What can I do to avoid getting involved in dead-end relationships in the future? Is my need to be part of a couple a cover-up for not dealing with my commitment issues?" Once you've answered some of these questions, you can either choose to stay in the relationship to work through your issues or leave in order to gain some clarity. Either way, you'll have a better understanding of what's keeping you from taking the next step forward.

THE DOCTOR IS IN

You can't be in a good, healthy, happy, mutual, interdependent, supportive relationship until you know who you are. That's the first and most essential step to eventually becoming part of a committed relationship. And how do you do that? Well, the most obvious way is going into personal therapy: getting to know your inner world, getting to know your emotions, your frailties, your strengths, really knowing yourself deeply. Because when you know yourself deeply, you really know whether or not you want to be in a committed relationship. You can't just make the assumption that you want to be.

—Allison Moir-Smith, M.A.

THE LONG-DISTANCE RUNNER INSTANT RECAP

If you've missed any of the commitment pointers in this chapter, you may want to stick around for this quick recap.

- Long-Distance Runners enjoy all the benefits that come with relationships—support, security, affection—but don't like the icky commitment part of it.

- Boredom should be a sign to roll up your sleeves and start working on your relationship, not a sign to abandon ship altogether.

- Constantly choosing relationships with built-in problems is one way to act out your commitment-phobic patterns.

- Just because you've spent a lot of time with your guy doesn't mean you're capable of making a commitment to him.

- If you're not comfortable talking about commitment after several years of dating, do yourself and your partner a favor and figure out what you're so afraid of.

- Keeping one foot out the door may be a person's way of saying, "I love you, I enjoy having you in my life, but I'm scared of committing to you."

- You may enjoy being in relationships, but that doesn't necessarily mean you're good at commitment.

- Some Long-Distance Runners pick partners who are truly incompatible so they have a ready-made excuse once they've decided to leave.

- No matter how wonderful it feels, being in a relationship doesn't prove that you're special, witty, or lovely.

- If you're always going from one liaison to another and have never spent any amount of time getting to know yourself, you may not be ready to make a permanent commitment.

10

Get Over It!

Whether you've found out you're a fun but flighty Free Spirit, an intrepid Tinker Bell, a drowning Damsel, a sassy Serial Dater, a prowling Player, a Long-Distance runner, a fastidious Nitpicker, or a little of all of these, by now you probably have a better idea of where you stand on the commitment meter, and I hope you have greater insight into your issues.

While increasing awareness is a crucial part of the equation, where would you be if I just left you hanging? After all, many of you are probably thinking: "Yep, that's me. I totally recognize myself in this book. But now what? Is there any hope for getting over these issues?" The answer to that is a resounding yes!

One of the first two skills you'll learn will be how to reduce your vulnerability to fears and manage runaway emotions. You'll also find some advice for helping you to look at commitment in a more positive way. In this day and age, it's very easy to get cynical and focus on the drawbacks of a committed relationship rather than its rewards. But even if you're not prepared to go from an Ambivalent Annie to a Committed Cindy quite yet, this general overview will outline the six most common mistakes commitment-phobic women make. So once you are ready to change your commitment-shy ways, you'll have everything you need to help you do just that.

What's more, you'll find basic strategies that will help you cope with your anxiety, whether you're single and dating, in a long-term relationship, cohabiting, or careening toward a wedding. No matter what commitment category you fall into, it's important to realize that with a little hard work, some determination, and a lot of soul-searching, you can learn to control your anxiety. Hoping, wishing, and praying that your commitment issues will disappear are just not enough. You need to dedicate yourself to working on them day in and day out. Not to say that you'll ever be free of the commitment-phobia bug entirely, but you will have a better understanding of how to manage your commitment-phobia so it doesn't play games with your head, wreck your relationships, and take over your life.

STUCK IN MY HEAD: CURBING OVERANALYSIS AND INDECISIVENESS

We've all been there. One minute you're certain he's the one for you, and the next minute you're convinced you're about to make the biggest mistake of your life. With so many choices to make and our fear of making the wrong one, many of us develop paralysis, unable to make any definitive moves without constantly second-guessing ourselves. The fear of making a bad decision is one of the most common traits that all commitment-phobes share. So whether you're trying to pick out a keeper from a sea of available suitors or have to make a decision whether to get married, here are some tips that will make the process a whole lot smoother.

1. Don't Overresearch

When it comes to commitment-phobia, it's important that you understand that overresearching your options (serial dating, over-analyzing your relationship, taking online compatibility tests) is a major pitfall. It's very easy to get stuck in the data collection phase and procrastinate making a decision. For instance, while it's important to have a point of comparison for the guys you're seeing, going on twenty dates or more every month is definitely taking the research thing too far. The same goes for those of you investigating your partners. There's a point beyond which analyzing him further only creates problems where none existed. After all, no one looks good when placed under a microscope, and it may lead you to exaggerate flaws that you would have otherwise

Elina Furman

glossed over. So while it's important to be informed about his strengths and weaknesses, you don't have to subject him to a battery of psychological testing and background checks to feel confident in your decision.

THE CONFESSIONAL: Marni, 32

I've noticed in my life that I am really good at making big decisions when it turns out that I knew somewhere inside that it's what I want. If I'm having problems making big decisions and I'm on the fence, it's kind of a red flag for me. If I'm not sure about something, that usually translates into I probably should not do it, should not buy it, or whatever the case may be.

2. Forget Your Gut

That sounds crazy, right? For years, we've been hearing about women's intuition and how important it is for us to trust our gut instincts. But for those of you with commitment-phobia, trusting your gut may be the most dangerous thing you can do.

One of the biggest mistakes many of you make is thinking that any uncertainty, however slight, is a sign that your relationship is doomed to failure. So when a little doubt creeps in, you take it for a gut instinct and a sign to escape from whatever commitment you're in. You think, "If I'm so confused, that must mean something is wrong with my relationship. Shouldn't I just know if it's right?"

While gut instinct is an important component in decision making, for women with commitment-phobia the issue is far more complex than a tingling in the stomach. Many of you are just anxious people in general and it may be hard for you to determine how you feel about anything in your life. After all, your instincts are probably all jumbled up from going through the overanalysis spin cycle.

There's a large contingent of those who believe in the motto "If in doubt, don't do it." Honestly, I don't know where this idea got started. I suspect it sprang from those women who are constantly harping on how they just *knew* their guy was "the one" on the first date. Try to avoid these women and the whole business of "just knowing" altogether. Someone as complicated and conflicted as you are has enough issues without this additional pressure of needing total certainty. Bottom line: just because you feel some hesitation or a warning from your gut, that doesn't mean that the relationship is going to fail. In fact, indecision and anxiety are a very normal part of making a commitment to someone. If you weren't a little uncertain, then you'd have something to worry about!

3. Just Do It

While I would never tell you to throw yourself into a decision without weighing up all the pros and cons, overresearching your options may lead to a lifetime of vacillation, fear, and emotional paralysis. So how do you learn to make good decisions? Well, you start by mastering the 80 percent rule. Face the fact that there's never going to be a time when you're 100 percent certain of anything. So if you're 80 percent sure that the person you're with will make a good partner, then that's all the certainty you're ever going to get.

Once you've determined whether you're 80 percent confident, it may be time to take some good old-fashioned action. Be conscious, be circumspect, and be careful, but take the leap. As with any phobia, be it insects or heights, we often have to face what scares us the most in order to conquer our fears. So it should come as no surprise that one of the best cures for commitment anxiety is just to make a commitment.

And if you make a mistake? Well, so be it. After all, one of the ways we learn to trust our instincts is through hindsight, by looking back at those things we could have done differently. In the end, following the 80 percent rule of thumb will help you take calculated risks, not reckless ones. So if you've checked the depth of the pool, stuck your toe in the water, and held your finger in the wind to see which way it's blowing, there's a good chance that it's safe to dive in.

THE CONFESSIONAL: Ellen, 37

The reason I have a hard time making commitments is because of my indecisiveness. Sometimes I have a fear of making the wrong decision. But sometimes you have to make a decision and just throw yourself into it and see what comes of it. Sometimes pure avoidance of marriage or commitment isn't necessarily the answer. I don't think it's realistic to think that something better is going to come along. Just like with everything else, you actually are better off making a decision, getting into a commitment, and seeing if it works out rather than waiting for the next person to come along.

THE PANIC ROOM:
MANAGING RUNAWAY EMOTIONS

Right now, a large majority of you are probably freaking out about what all this means for your future commitment prospects. You may even feel that by reading this book you've opened the equivalent of a Pandora's box. Whether you're distressed about settling down, breaking up, or spending the rest of your life alone, here's a quick primer for breaking the panic cycle.

1. Make Friends with Your Anxiety

One of the biggest pitfalls many of you will face is believing that your commitment anxiety is somehow abnormal, atypical, unusual, or uncommon. As a result, you often fight against and deny the uncomfortable feelings, hoping that they will just disappear one day. The most important thing you can do is accept your commitment fears as a natural and normal part of your life, much like sleeping, eating, and breathing. Sometimes just realizing that millions of other women suffer from the same chronic commitment stress can be enough to make you feel better.

The next time you feel scared, anxious, or confused, sit down and try to quiet your mind. Try to pinpoint what set you off— whether it was a disagreement with your partner or something going on in your own life. Once you've done that, take long deep breaths and just observe those negative emotions. Trying to run away or denying your feelings will only make matters worse.

Another key thing to remember is that your doubts about your partner will come and go. You're not always going to feel madly in love or 100 percent certain about him. In fact, there will be many times when, out of the blue, you feel like bolting. But that's only to be expected. The last thing you'll want to do is act on those temporary feelings.

2. Avoid the Crystal Ball

If you're on the brink of becoming exclusive, cohabiting, or getting married to someone, it's all too easy to panic and wonder, "But how will I feel one year, five years, or ten years from now?" After all, people change, right? How do you know you will feel exactly the same way five years from now? The answer is: you don't!

No matter how tempting it is to worry about the future of your relationship, you have to accept that there is absolutely no guarantee that things will work out. Worrying about the future is one way to avoid making a decision. No matter how many psychics or astrologers you visit, no one can tell you what to do with your life or what the future holds. In the end, the best thing you can do is focus on the present. Ask yourself: "Am I getting what I want out of the relationship at this exact moment?" If the answer is yes (or 80 percent yes), rest assured the prognosis is as good as it's going to get.

THE CONFESSIONAL: Samir, 26

I'd been living with Kyle for about one year when he asked me to marry him. Our relationship always had some ups and downs. We always quarreled over little things—you know, like who would take out the trash and his being late all the time. But nothing that was a deal breaker or anything. In fact, I was really happy most of the time. So when he asked me, I said yes. Not too long after that I started having all these doubts. I would wake up in the middle of the night freaking out about the future, like what if we grew apart? Or what if we fell out of love? Or what if we ended up miserable together? You could say the whole engagement became a nightmare for me. Finally, I talked to this one married friend who told me that I was being silly with all my worries. She said we never know what's going to happen, and that it's better to focus on the here and now than to project my fears into the future. Once I stopped focusing on what would happen or what could go wrong, I was much happier and things got better for us.

3. Give Yourself a Break

Too many women spend their entire lives obsessing about relationships—not having one, not wanting one, not being able to sustain one. So when they finally do get married or committed, many of them wish they had taken that time to enjoy their single years.

As you read this book, many of you will unearth your hidden desire for commitment, and I hope you will come away with a better understanding of what's been standing in your way. Others of you, however, will discover that you're not ready to make a serious commitment. And there will be some of you who will still go into denial mode and redouble your dating efforts in order to avoid facing the reality that you may need to be alone for a while. But don't get caught in this trap. While realizing that you're a long way away from forming a lasting connection can indeed be scary, don't ever criticize or berate yourself for not being ready.

Choosing to be single is a tough and often unpopular stance. So it's no surprise that many of us make this choice unconsciously yet continue to act as if we're looking for a commitment. The most important thing to remember is that not all of us are prepared to make a lifelong commitment by the time we turn 30. Some of us will take longer than others to get to this point. But no matter how horrible it's making you feel right now, consciously choosing to be single for a while is one of the greatest gifts you can give yourself. So if you find that you're not quite ready to throw yourself into deep commitment waters, give yourself a break and say, "I'm single right now and that's just fine with me!"

FRIENDS OR FOES: DEALING WITH COMMITMENT SABOTEURS

It's only natural that the people we lean on most—parents, friends, siblings—are also the ones who can drive us the craziest. As well-meaning as many of them are, sometimes our support network has a way of unleashing the most vehement commitment-phobes in us. Remember that even the best-intentioned people, no matter how much they care about us, can sometimes do more harm than good.

1. Recognize Toxic Friends

Whether all your girlfriends are single and think no guy is good enough for you or are happily married and believe anyone who doesn't walk down the aisle is secretly crying into her pillow every night, it's important to be wary of toxic friends.

When it comes to your single friends, many of them have a stake in keeping you single. After all, whom will they go out on the town with or call in the middle of the night once you're happily ensconced in a committed relationship? Oftentimes, there's an unspoken pressure among single girlfriends to remain single, whether it manifests as criticizing each other's dates or saying backhanded things about marriage, couples, and commitment. It's only natural for them to act out and try to keep you single as long as possible. Of course, those perky committed friends who are constantly pestering you ("So when are you going to get hitched?") are hardly off the hook, either. You may get so infuriated with them that you decide to avoid commitment indefinitely, lest you end up becoming as annoying as they are.

The most important thing to remember is that no matter how

much you rely on your support network for moral support, your friends have plenty of issues and insecurities that have nothing to do with you. The best thing you can do is not join either camp—anti-commitment or pro-commitment—and just focus on figuring out what's right for you.

THE CONFESSIONAL: Karen, 29

All my single friends were notorious partiers. They moved in kind of a fast set—lots of money, parties, drugs, et cetera. One day, I was having trouble with a current boyfriend and decided to go out with my friends for a night on the town. It was horrible! It was like they all ganged up on me and decided to do an intervention or something. They kept telling me how I was wasting my life being with this guy and how it was embarrassing for them to hang out with us together. Finally, I just had enough. My boyfriend may not have been rich or cool by their standards, but he treated me really well and I loved him. I realized that part of the trouble in our relationship was that my boyfriend knew my friends hated him. In the end, I decided that I couldn't continue being friends with them. Not only because I was becoming serious about my boyfriend, but because I didn't like what they stood for.

FRIEND OR FOE?

If you're having a hard time spotting who might be a toxic single friend, these telltale signs are bound to clear up any confusion.

1. She doesn't want to talk about anything other than your love life.

2. She says negative things about your mutual friends who are married.

3. She finds minor flaws with your boyfriends and harps on them when you're out with friends.

4. She plays therapist to the point where you feel you have to make up problems just to please her.

5. She talks badly about her dates and men in general.

6. She gives you backhanded compliments such as "I wish I could be as easy to please as you are."

7. She often tells you how your boyfriend doesn't deserve you.

8. She is always in the throes of some romantic crisis, so you never have time to deal with your own issues.

9. She makes snide comments such as "I give it three months" when you tell her you're in love.

10. She brings up topics you're uncomfortable with (weight, past breakups, and other secret vulnerabilities) when you get into fights with her.

2. Keep Your Own Counsel

Whether it's your single friends pressuring you to break up with a nice guy you've been seeing, the cubicle-mate who thinks *Redbook* is a dating bible, or your parents constantly asking you when you'll get married, it's all too easy to lose sight of where you stand in the commitment conundrum. The reason many of us have become so commitment-phobic is that there are just too many people telling us how we should feel, act, and think. It's no wonder we don't trust those voices in our heads, since we really have no clue whom they belong to.

But how much are we responsible for letting all these people feel as if they have a say in our love lives? After all, the only way for other people to impact you is if you invite them into your world. Not to say that you shouldn't share intimate things about yourself or ask others for advice, but it's important to practice some discretion. So instead of telling everyone within earshot about your latest love problems, designate one person whom you trust to be your sounding board. As tempting as it is to call three friends, your mom, and your siblings when you have a love crisis, part of becoming commitment-ready is learning to stand on your own two feet and make the tough decisions all by yourself.

THE CONFESSIONAL: Nadine, 34

I have a mother who thinks I should get married. And I live in the South, where it's almost unheard of if you are 34 and you've never been married. Down here, if you are 34 you usually have two ex-husbands, maybe one from high school, and three kids from the two different husbands. You kind of tend to get the "What's wrong with you?" questions, "Why haven't you been able to attract a guy?" when in fact that has not been the problem.

3. Find Commitment Role Models

Role models! Where are they when you need them? Because so many of us didn't grow up with positive relationship examples, we simply do not know what a healthy commitment looks like. There's your best friend, who's on her third marriage; your mother, who is carrying on a secret online love affair; and the constant celebrity breakups that leave you wondering whether all relationships are doomed from the start. And when it comes to some of your married friends—well, that won't do, either, considering how annoyingly "smug married" some of them are. Between all their talk of their houses in the country and having to check with their husbands about every minor decision, it's no wonder you're terrified of ending up like them. With such an absence of positive role models, it should come as no surprise that we have so many issues. It's all too easy to become a bit cynical, thinking the world is just not conducive to happy and smug-free relationships.

If you're serious about making a commitment, it's important

that you find a committed friend or a couple whom you respect and admire. Granted, finding a cool couple that you can hang with can be difficult, but you'll have to try. Whether it's an aunt, a family friend, or just someone you've met and are inspired by, try to spend time with them and find out how they've been able to make commitment look sexy, exciting, and, most importantly, possible.

THE DOCTOR IS IN

Children of divorce, in my experience, have an additional barrier or hurdle to cross in that they didn't grow up in a functioning, lasting marriage. And they don't have any model, at least in the household that they grew up in, of a relationship that works. So children of divorce, daughters of divorce, need to look outward in their community of friends and to other marriages to find an idea of what might work. Maybe they have an aunt or uncle, a colleague, or an older friend. They have to find other images to help them out.

—*Allison Moir-Smith, M.A.*

FAULTY WIRING: FIXING NEGATIVE COMMITMENT SCRIPTS

Whether it's our views on politics, religion, or commitment, we rarely take the time to really look at when or how many of our worldviews first formed. So it may come as a surprise to find out that many of you are carrying around negative commitment scripts that may be deeply buried beneath the surface. And while you may have great reasons for believing what you do, it's important to analyze and update your views every now and then to reflect who you are today.

1. Eliminate the Traitor Complex

Many of us were raised on the do-anything-and-be-anyone-you-want-to feminist motto. As a result, we worry about breaking the unwritten rules of feminism, feeling like huge sellouts if we even so much as think about an engagement ring or the prospect of trying on wedding dresses. The idea of getting married or making a commitment can make us feel as if we're turning our backs on all those hardworking women who championed our rights to vote, work, and hold public office. We feel guilty about wanting to settle down. We feel guilty about wanting to take some time off from work. We feel guilty . . . Well, you get the idea.

Many of us have a hard time reconciling our feminist ideals with commitment and marriage. But remember that while honoring your feminist roots is important, your first duty should be to yourself. After all, one of the main objectives of the feminist movement was about giving us the right to choose a life that makes us happy, whether that be living on your own as a single, shacking up, or getting married. So if you haven't figured out exactly what scenario will make you happiest, consider that your next feminist imperative.

2. Give Yourself Permission to Change

Whether you're a die-hard commitment-phobe or are just generally ambivalent, it's important to reevaluate your commitment perspective now and then. While you may have spent the first thirty years of your life imagining yourself as a sophisticated single gal about town, going to museums and organizing charity events, it's okay to change course and come up with an alternative vision of your future. Or if you always pictured yourself traveling to distant lands and helping underprivileged kids, that doesn't mean you can't update your mental picture to include commitment. Just because when you were younger you swore that you would never get married, that doesn't mean you can't change your mind.

When it comes to your views about commitment, the most important thing you can do is stay flexible. Even if you've spent half your life railing against the tyranny of couplehood and ranting about how annoying married people are, you can gradually shift your outlook to reflect the changes you've gone through. Consistency may be great when it comes to your work ethic or family relationships, but it's important to know when an idea has outworn its welcome, especially if circumstances, such as meeting someone you really care about, warrant a reappraisal.

3. Stop Rebelling

There are innumerable ways to get turned off to commitment. What with all those people asking you why you're still single, the wedding industry raking in $70 billion a year, and the new "opt-out revolution" for working moms that seems to romanticize the stifling 1950s, it's no wonder we're feeling iffy about the whole thing. In fact, pressure from the media, friends, and family can become so grating that it can lead us to adopt a negative attitude about commitment as an act of rebellion.

Remember when your parents forbade you to stay out late and you rebelled against them just to prove a point? Or when they decreed you couldn't wear makeup, and you ended up piling it on at school and looking ridiculous in the process? As natural as our rebellion is, there's a point where it can do more harm than good.

Just because everyone is hassling you about being single or extolling the virtues of commitment doesn't mean you should take on a defiant attitude and just dismiss the whole thing. If you do that, the only person you're rebelling against will be yourself. You may not agree with the prevailing conventional notions about commitment, but that doesn't mean you have to reject the whole concept outright. There may be some good things about commitment, provided you take the time to analyze your personal views and reject the parts you don't like. So when in doubt, don't let extreme pressure tactics force you to adopt a diametrically opposed point of view about commitment that may not even be your own.

4. Start Settling Up

Don't you just hate the phrase "settling down"? Can you think of anything less exciting? "Settle down"—that's what my second-grade teacher told us when we would get a little too rowdy in class. Goodbye, fun, joie de vivre, and feeling alive; it's time to settle down. Or what about terms such as *marital institution* and even *wife*, for that matter? Whether you automatically think of straitjackets or of being pregnant and baking cookies in the kitchen, many of us have very negative reactions to these words and may not even be aware of it.

If you're going to change your negative attitude toward commitment, you'll first have to become aware of what expressions trigger your commitment panic. Some words are just full of scary connotations. That's why it's important to redefine what commitment means to you and find some better terminology that doesn't make you want to hurl every time you hear it. Here is some commitment-friendly lingo that can help you change your tune.

Commitment-Scary	Commitment-Friendly
Settling down	Settling up
Compromise	Artful negotiation
Committed	Devoted
Little wife	Partner in crime
Husband	Stud boy
Wedlock	Lip lock

THE CONFESSIONAL: Amy, 28

When I first got married, I was terrified of saying the word husband. *My dad wasn't the greatest father in the world, and every time my mom said the word* husband *her face would just kind of drop. I guess I associated it with being unhappy and miserable. Funny thing, my husband had no problem with it. He would just go around and say proudly, "This is my wife," but I still kept introducing him as my significant other. It hurt me that I couldn't return the favor. Finally, we agreed that I could call him whatever I wanted. In fact, he encouraged me to come up with a nickname that worked better for me. I guess just having that pressure off me gave me the courage to start saying it.*

WOULD YOU DATE YOU? THE BITCH FACTOR

One of the top ways commitment-phobes act out their ambivalence is by getting involved in relationships and then sabotaging the union so they don't have to commit. Whether it's fighting, criticizing, or withholding sex, some of us start out great in the relationship, only to end up acting like a royal pain in the neck to get our boyfriends to break up with us. So once the relationship is over, we never have to admit that we were responsible for the breakup. Pretty sneaky, huh?

Of course, most of us are completely unaware of this behavior. So while it may be hard for you to admit that you're far from perfect in the relationship department, you'll have to do just that if you want to have any hope of getting over your commitment issues.

THE DOCTOR IS IN

One very good strategy for a woman who is afraid of being in an intimate relationship or committing is to chase the man away through what's commonly called being a "bitch." She can be so demanding and

Elina Furman

so difficult to please that the man gives up and says, "You're right. I'm not good enough. I can't please you no matter what I do."

—*Dr. Deborah Anapol*

1. Combating Selfishness

The reason I can safely say that many of us long-term singles have a tendency to be self-oriented is because I know myself all too well. Not that I'm a total narcissist or anything, but calling home when I'm late and not automatically reaching for the last chicken wing when I'm hungry are skills that took time to master. And when I say selfish, I really do mean that in the nicest way. Despite the fact that many of us singletons volunteer our time, selflessly give to charities, and are very generous tippers, the more time we spend on our own the harder it becomes for us to go from a "me" mind-set to a "we" mentality. Looking out for your own interests is important when you're single, but when you're in a relationship, the same behavior can be detrimental.

It's extremely important to realize that the skills you learn while single are not the same as those needed to make a relationship work. But it's not as hard to change self-centered behavior as you think. It's just a matter of practice. Once you work on compromising and doing caring things for your partner, it will eventually become second nature to the point where you don't even think twice about it. In the end, it's all how you look at it. Just turn the M in *me* upside down, and you end up with *we*.

THE CONFESSIONAL: Meryl, 47

Internally you have to give up some stuff in order to be with someone else because they become a really important piece of you, so you are always going to lose part of yourself. But I struggle with remaining independent and trying to stay true to myself and not lose too much of

> myself. I'm still coping with the fear. You always have to take that other
> person into consideration—common courtesy kind of stuff. Even
> though I feel like I have my independence and that I try to balance as
> well as I can, when you are in a relationship it's a responsibility. Now I
> feel okay enough to say, "I'm going out with so-and-so tonight; what
> are you doing?" I'm okay with saying, "I have this and this planned,
> and it's just for me."

2. Miss Control Freak

Okay, so men can sometimes act like dominating control freaks, but it's important to note how often we're guilty of the same offense. Picking fights, acting moody, and making your partner feel like he's always doing something wrong is a great way to get someone to break up with you. In fact, that's exactly what many of you do so you can get out of the relationship, avoid commitment, and never have to take personal responsibility for your own issues.

Many of us commitment-phobes have a perfectionistic streak that makes us try to control every aspect of the relationship. Unless our partner fits some preconceived mold, we feel we can't possibly commit to him. Whether it's his sloppy ways or inability to dress himself, it can be all too tempting to want to change him or control the relationship. Of course, if you're not ready to commit, no one will ever be good enough for you. So either accept your partner for who he is or leave the relationship altogether.

3. Bad Fighting

All of us have been guilty of this at one point or another. For instance, every time my fiancé and I had a fight, I would start to plan an escape route, browse apartment ads online, or imagine myself moving to another country. Many of you are probably guilty of the same things—threatening to break up, hurling insults you can't take back, and doing other things that show you're not in this for the long haul. And while all couples will fight from time to time, *how* you fight says more about your commitment level than anything else. Bad fighting can be very damaging to a relationship. In fact, constantly threatening to break up whenever you have a fight can keep a relationship from developing a stable foundation.

If you do find yourself in the middle of a heated exchange, don't use your commitment fears as leverage in the relationship. Telling your partner you're afraid of commitment just keeps him on his toes, which you might actually wish to do, since it gets you what you want. Commitment is about holding tough and being loyal during the good and the bad times. So instead of threatening to jump ship whenever things don't go your way, deal with your own moods and anxiety without taking it out on your boyfriend.

4. The Case of the Roving Eye

Whether it's your personal trainer, that cute new coworker in the next cubicle, or even his best friend, it's not at all uncommon for those of you on the brink of commitment to suddenly find yourself forming crushes on everyone in sight. You can have the best relationship with your guy, but as soon as the concept of commitment is introduced, you may find yourself powerfully drawn to someone new. While this is extremely normal, many of you will freak out, thinking that your newfound attraction is a sign that something is wrong with your relationship.

Whether you are happy in your relationship or not, it's entirely natural to be attracted to other people. Admit it—attractive and interesting people are just fun to be around. There is absolutely no reason to feel guilty for having these feelings. And as fun as it is to flirt with someone who's different from your partner, it's important to realize that it's the very newness that attracts you.

Forming crushes is by no means an indicator that you don't love your partner. What's interesting is that most of you will never act on your urges. In fact, it's a safe way to play out some of your fantasies without ever hurting anyone, provided you don't succumb to temptation, of course. So remember: being attracted to other people is not a sign your relationship is damaged, it's a sign that you're normal!

5. Roll Up Your Sleeves

Many women say, "If my relationship is this much work, it must not be right." Ask anyone who has been in an "easy" relationship and they'll tell you that everything may go perfectly smoothly for a while, but when you hit the brick wall (and all relationships invariably do), your union won't stand a fighting chance.

The problem with easy relationships is that they don't teach us how to negotiate, set boundaries, and work out kinks before they become full-fledged problems. In easy relationships, it's all too easy to coast along, never developing the skills you need to keep your union fresh, alive, and exciting. On the flip side, if you're in a dynamic, challenging relationship with two head-strong people, you're going to learn a lot about how to fulfill your own needs while still maintaining the needs of the partnership. As tough as the going may seem for a while, the lessons you learn may carry you forward for years to come. And while fighting every day isn't necessarily a good sign, being challenged and pushing each other to be better can keep the relationship stronger. Some relationships may in fact be harder than others, but they may also be more worthy of the extra effort.

THE CONFESSIONAL: Gail, 28

The fear of being with one person for the rest of your life is still there, but I think that's natural and that's okay. When you're in a relationship with someone, you start to really invest and care, and you count on them caring about you. And that kind of makes you think about commitment. And it's scary because it takes a lot of work. I'm at the beginning of the relationship right now and we've already had issues come up. But it's normal. It's work to stay in a relationship and keep it strong. Really communicating and being open and honest is hard, but worth it.

Elina Furman

6. Don't Blame Your Partner for Your Issues

One of the biggest mistakes many commitment-phobes make is to blame their dissatisfaction with themselves, their careers, and their lives in general on their partners. If you're depressed about something—whether it's your job or your family—it's all too tempting to generalize those feelings to include your relationship. And when you do mix up these issues, it's very tempting to think that if you got out of this relationship, then you would feel better. I've seen too many women, myself included, let a relationship go down the drain thinking that doing so would somehow improve their lives. But don't confuse your dissatisfaction with your life with dissatisfaction with your partner. In the end, ending your relationship won't fix your problems; it will just give you new problems to deal with.

MY SO-CALLED SINGLE LIFE: COMMITMENT-FRIENDLY LIVING

Being commitment-ready is a state of mind. It means having self-knowledge, realistic expectations, and the willingness to compromise in order to make a relationship work. And while many of you think you're ready now (and your dedication to finishing this book speaks volumes), a few extra pointers never hurt anyone.

1. Make Room

While it's important to have a balanced and full life, many women overdo it, trying to create an image of the ultra-fabulous, über-busy single. It may be impressive that you have a gazillion friends, invitations to the hottest parties, and unique hobbies, but if you don't make some room in your life for a committed relationship, don't be surprised if it keeps eluding you.

Think of it like this: once you make room on a table and clear all the stuff away, something new is bound to appear on it. This rule applies to everything. If you're obsessed with your pet, work 24/7, are absorbed in your children, have a bed that only fits one person, or are a clutter bug who's embarrassed to bring people home, you probably don't have as much time or space for a committed relationship as you think. So if you fit any of these categories, it may just be time to clean up your act and make some physical, emotional, and psychological room in your life.

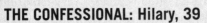

THE CONFESSIONAL: Hilary, 39

Career has always been very important to me. I've probably made decisions that favored my work over relationships just because I feel like I am solely responsible for my financial future. I have seen many cases where women made themselves financially dependent on a partner only to be divorced later. The guys I've dated have always had their own careers and pursuits, but there were times when I would have to stay late at the job and not see them as often as they wanted me to. So I'm actually making a career choice that will allow me to be a lot more flexible in my career and have more free time, because I do see that as a possible stumbling block in the future.

2. Don't Become a Commitment Cynic

While no one is saying you should spend every moment fantasizing about being part of a twosome, it's important to maintain a certain optimism despite all the setbacks and commitment gripes you've acquired over the years. As the ultimate cynic, I know how hard it is to keep any kind of faith in commitment and love in the face of all the contrary evidence. With so many strikes against relationships and marriage, it can be too easy to become disillusioned about the whole business. But if you're going to change your attitude, it's important that you not buy in to the negative myths about commitment (such as all couples being boring, annoying, and smug).

You should also avoid talking negatively about commitment. Instead of letting your fears and hang-ups drive you to make anti-commitment statements, you may want to analyze when it was exactly that you first banned committed relationships from your life.

Was it after a bad breakup? Was it during a confrontation in childhood? Was it a reaction to social pressure from your family, friends, and coworkers? Once you figure out where your decision sprang from, you'll be able to realize whether your cynical position is a front to keep yourself from getting hurt or a legitimate stance on relationships, marriage, and lifelong commitment.

AN ODE TO COMMITMENT

Not to sound like the National Marriage Project or anything, but it's important to remind ourselves of the positive aspects of commitment once in a while. Here are some benefits you may want to consider.

- **Steady Sex.** While it's great to be able to experiment with different partners when you're single, there's something comforting about knowing where your next meal is coming from. In fact, Linda J. Waite, a University of Chicago scholar and author of the book *The Case for Marriage,* claims that the sex lives of committed and married partners are far better than those of singles.

- **More Green Stuff.** Committed couples not only have more love to spread around, they also have more cash. It's been reported that people in stable, committed relationships have higher incomes than singles.

- **Touchy-Feely.** Constant hugs, emotional support, and feeling all warm inside—you can't underestimate the importance of this stuff.

- **Stability.** While stability has become a dirty word, it's really not as boring as it seems. In fact, a committed relationship can give you the freedom to pursue other exciting hobbies and interests (other than dating, of course).

- **Friend in Need.** No matter how much we play the loner card, most of us are social animals who thrive on human companionship. In healthy committed relationships, partners serve as each other's primary social outlet and closest friend.

- **Happy Pill.** You're much less likely to go berserk or suffer from depression if you're in a committed relationship, at least according to a new study conducted by researcher Claire Kamp Dush, a postdoctoral fellow at the Institute for Social Sciences at Cornell University. The study found that having a committed romantic relationship makes both men and women happier and far less likely to go crazy.

- **Health Perks.** There are some studies that say people who are married are generally healthier than those who are not. According to a 2004 report from the Centers for Disease Control and Prevention, married adults are sprightlier than their divorced, widowed, or never-married adult counterparts.

3. Keep Learning and Teaching

One of the most common mistakes many women make is underplaying their commitment issues. After all, many of you didn't even know you suffered from this anxiety until reading this book. Even now, some of you may be tempted to sweep it all under a rug and hope that your commitment ambivalence will just work itself out. Problem is, the more you avoid dealing with these issues, the more entrenched your fears will become.

Once you've laid this book down, the most important thing you can do is continue working on your fears, insecurities, and hang-ups regarding permanence. After all, getting over your commitment issues is a gradual process that can take years of hard work and dedication. Even if you feel you're completely in the clear, you never know when the commitment monster will creep back in. That's why it's so important to stay vigilant through every step of your relationship. As hard as it is to admit this, ONCE A COMMITMENT-PHOBE, ALWAYS A COMMITMENT-PHOBE! The key is to become aware of your patterns so your issues don't disrupt your life or relationships. While reading this book and implementing the advice are solid steps in the right direction, you can't afford to get lax as you battle your commitment-phobia.

Once you've digested the information, your second goal should be to support and spread the word to other women. The reason why female commitment-phobia is such a problem is that most women don't know they're suffering from it. Our culture doesn't acknowledge these issues, so it is up to you to talk, explain, and share your experiences with other women. If you don't share your doubts, issues, and fears with one another, then many women will end up feeling alone and unsupported in their struggle to sustain a healthy committed relationship.

Just to create some guidelines, here are the top five things you should never say to or ask a female commitment-phobe.

1. **"Second thoughts mean it's not right."** Commitment-phobes have second thoughts about everything. Why shouldn't they have some doubts about their life partners?

2. **"I just *knew* he was the one."** Don't play revisionist history with your relationship. It's easy to say now that you knew, but if you look back, you'll see that things weren't always so clear.

3. **"Just listen to your gut."** Telling a commitment-phobic woman to listen to her gut is a recipe for disaster. Most can't tell the difference between their gut instinct and their commitment anxiety.

4. **"You should be happy, not freaking out."** Meeting someone you could potentially spend the rest of your life with is one of the most terrifying and exciting things that can happen. No wonder you're freaking out!

5. **"Is he 'the one'?"** What does that even mean, people?

And if you ever hear any of this drivel directed at you, don't freak out. Just laugh very loudly, as if they've just said the funniest thing in the world. If they press you, continue to laugh even harder. They'll probably wonder what in the world they said that was so funny, but don't bother explaining. Just consider it a private joke between you, me, and your fellow commitment-phobes.

Acknowledgments

First, I want to thank all the thoughtful, fascinating, and dynamic women who were brave enough to share their stories. Through everything, it was your voices and experiences that prodded me to continue. Your struggles, fears, and doubts helped me realize that we are not alone. I know your stories will be an inspiration for the many women struggling with these issues. For that, I will always be grateful.

I want to thank my mother, Mira, the ultimate free spirit, who inspires me by example and always believed in this project despite all odds. You taught me to never give up, and I'm so glad I didn't. My sister, Leah—thank you for always showing me that independence and freedom are their own rewards.

I would like to extend a deep gratitude to my editor, Amanda Patten, who understood where I was going even when I sometimes did not. Your pointed thoughts, comments, and suggestions inspired me to go deeper and try harder. To my agent, Laurie Abkemeier, who believed in this project from day one, thank you for all the time we spent talking about this book and the time you devoted to reading every word. I am lucky to consider you both my friends.

I would also like to thank the experts featured in this book who have contributed their time and wisdom.

- **Allison Moir-Smith, M.A.,** is a bridal counselor, psychotherapist, and author of *Emotionally Engaged: A Bride's Guide to Surviving the "Happiest" Time of Her Life.* Look for her book and Emotionally Engaged Bridal Counseling services offered at www.emotionallyengaged.com.

- **Debra Mandel, Ph.D.,** is a psychologist, columnist, speaker, media expert, and author of *Healing the Sensitive Heart* and two CDs, *Creating Healthy Boundaries in the*

Workplace and The Abuser Friendly Syndrome. Her latest book is titled *Your Boss Is Not Your Mother.* Visit her website at www.sensitiveheart.com.

- **Deborah Anapol, Ph.D.,** is the author of *The Seven Natural Laws of Love,* which can be found online at www.sevenlawsoflove.com. Leading seminars nationwide, she is also an inspiring and controversial speaker who has appeared on radio and television programs all across the USA and Canada.

- **Dr. Michael S. Broder** is the author of *Can Your Relationship Be Saved?: How to Know Whether to Stay or Go,* which can be found at www.drmichaelbroder.com.

To Rebecca, a recovering commitment-phobe, former boomeranger, my good friend, and researcher on this book, thank you for all your hard work. If it wasn't for your help, I honestly don't know how I would have finished it.

And finally, to Jay. You didn't give up on me and believed in us when I couldn't. When I can't find the words or the strength, you're always there. And that's commitment.

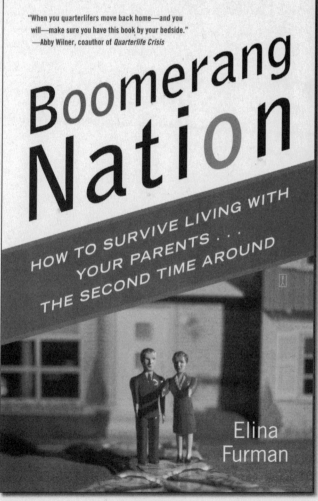